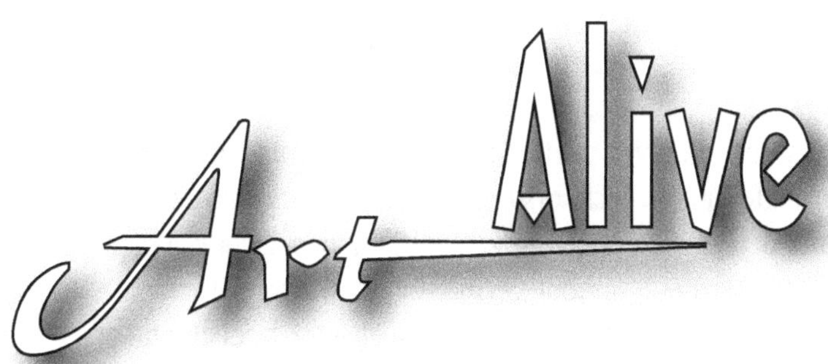

September through June

GRADES 4-5-6

ART ACTIVITIES
WITH GRADE LEVEL OBJECTIVES

by Syd Brown

ISBN 978-0-615-26166-9

Printed In the United States of America via Lulu Press

Publisher: Syd Brown Designs
656 Santa Lucia, Los Osos, California 93402

Art Alive

Seeing with new eyes through art.

First decide *why* you want the student to have art.

Then *what* it is you want them to learn.

Then *how* you will tell if it has happened.

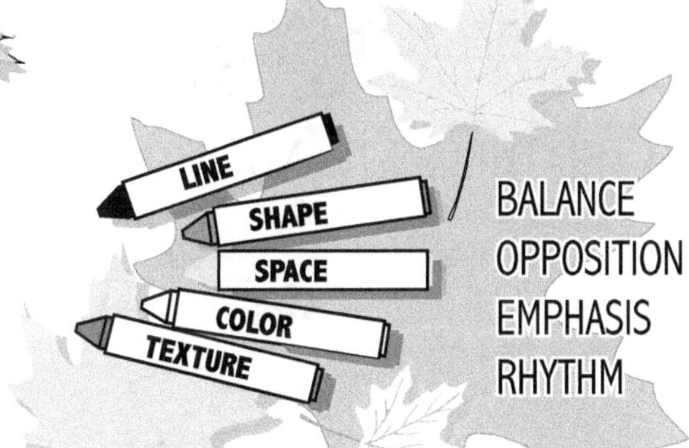

why: Art is a source of tools and skills for critical thinking. Creative thinking is basic to Art and Art is basic to creative thinking. Visual literacy in our world is as important as reading literacy. Art is basic to an appreciation of a quality life.

what: Art is observing, selecting elements, noticing similarities and differences. It is ordering, doing and most importantly, valuing. Art processes use the elements of line, shape, texture, space and color and mixes them with the principles of Balance, Opposition, Emphasis and Rhythm.

how: Art evaluation is not just the comparison of the student's old work to new, rather it looks to see if the student's use of an art vocabulary is growing and if the physical and skill levels are progressing. Evaluation looks to see if the student is becoming more aware of and expressive of the environment in art terms . It looks to see if the student is becoming more capable of expressing, making and acting on quality choices for the student's own life.

Looking at art and the world is easy if you have the right glasses

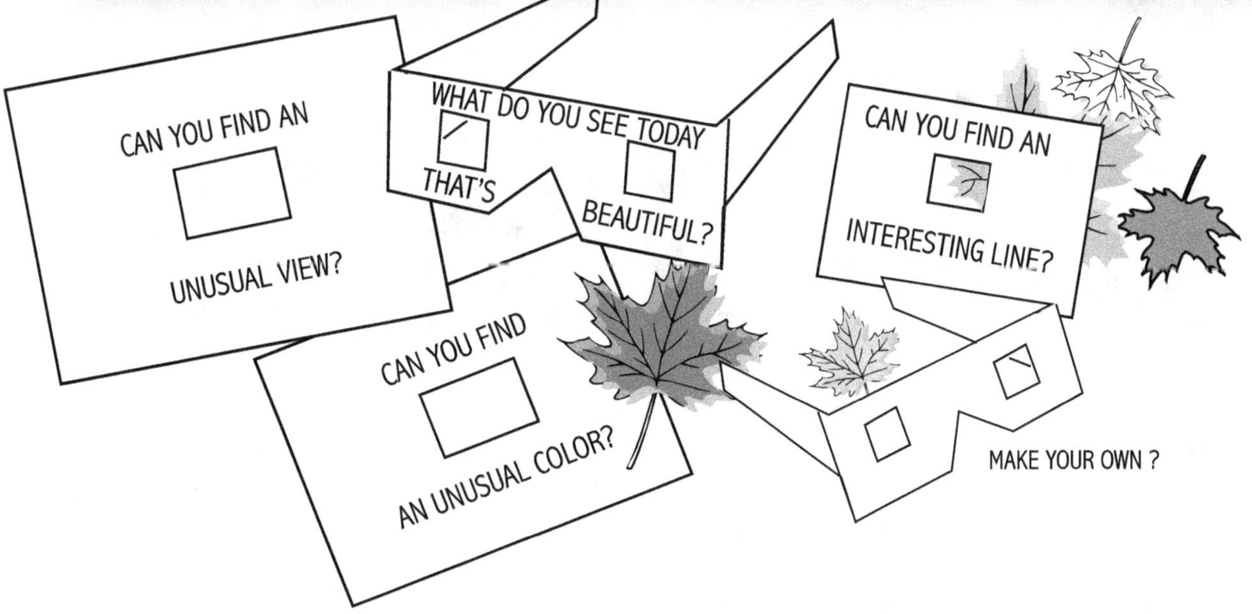

Art Alive
HOW DO WE BEGIN?

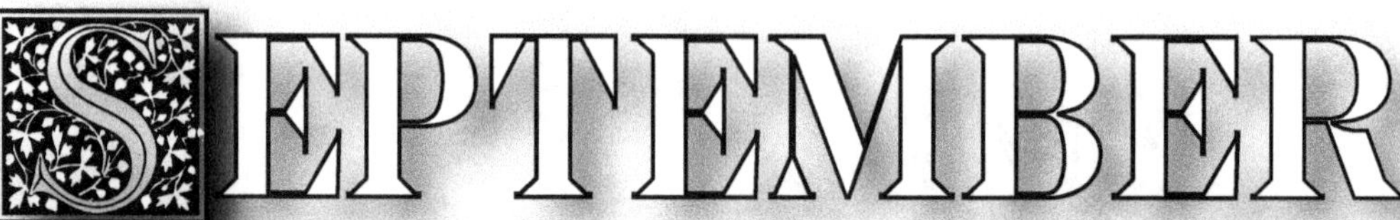

WITH THE THREE STRANDS (that's all there is to it!)

PERCEPTION

Analyzing, comparing, contrasting, encoding, and appreciation of things seen, touched, or heard.

EXPRESSION

Synthesizing new relationships, making personal statements about the world... as individual as our fingerprints.

AESTHETIC JUDGMENT

The valuing of the art elements as they interact through the principles of balance, rhythm, emphasis and opposition.

You get there with the elements!
You mix and match them with the principles.

Take a 3" x 3" square of cardboard. Draw a curve from one edge to another. Cut it out and use as a pattern. Make one row of designs on your paper and then turn it 90° and make another row of designs and turn it another 90° for another row. Continue with several rows turning 90° each time.

Use the same shape, cut another curve reflecting the first curve. Use both patterns. Change the colors on the new pattern row.

Look at Piet Mondrian's paintings. Talk about his use of balance and shape.

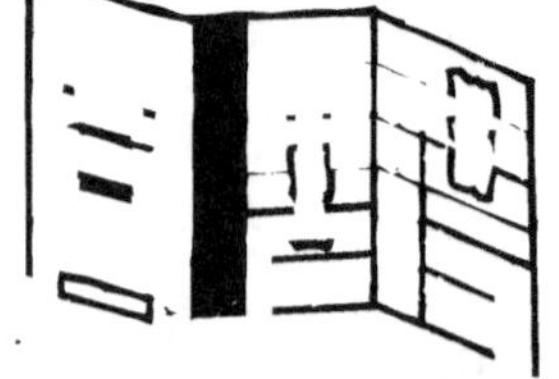

Cut seven rectangles from black paper, making sure that one of them is long enough to

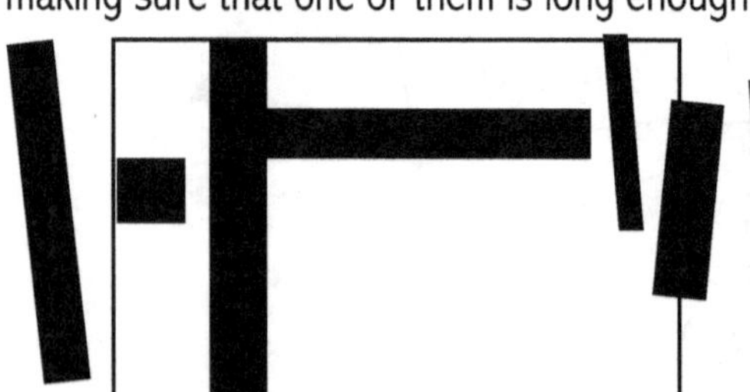

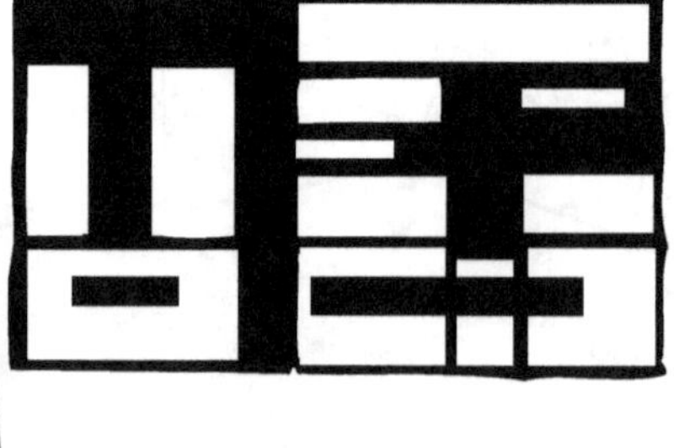

cross the page. Place these on your design in a manner that is pleasing to you. Do not paste yet. Turn your paper all directions. Is it balanced like a seesaw would be balanced? Continue until you are content with the balance of your design. Try another design with black and the primary colors (Red, yellow or blue), or just with the primary colors.

Draw the "yellow brick Road" on several numbered squares. Have as many friends as you want fill in the space on their square with creatures and without seeing the work of others. Reassemble.

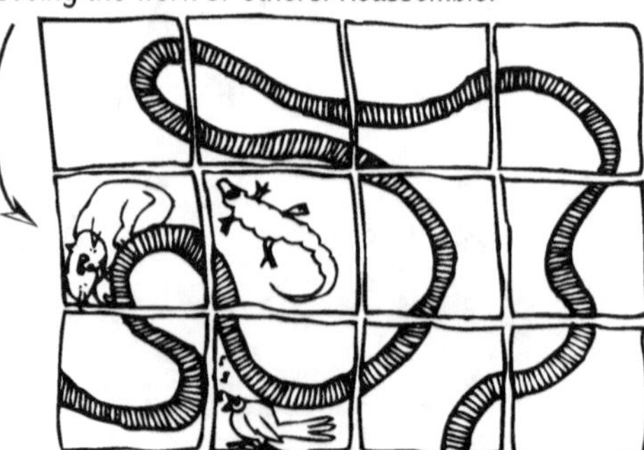

DESIGN IS BUILT ON BALANCE, VARIATION, AND EMPHASIS OF THE ELEMENTS.

You can make a "view" card from a 3 x 5 card by cutting a small hole in the center. Moving it closer to you or away from you changes what you see. A card can be made for anything you want to see...Line or shape or color.

Draw every day for 10 minutes. Drawing is thinking with a pencil. You need to practice drawing in your spare time. It will help you see the world and help you tell about the world.

Use a magnifying glass as a "view" card. Try anything to help you get a new view of the world.

PERCEPTION

Try new ways of seeing, look at out of focus slides, or through prisms, are what magnifying glasses. Pretend that you are from a different planet and are seeing this world for the first time.

Use newsprint and charcoal to make rubbings of tennis shoes. The flat side of a crayon works well, too.

Expression follows perceptions. Make it a tactile world. Make as many rubbings of textures as you can. Describe them as you make them. You're not through with art until you make aesthetic judgments about what you've done. Vocabulary terms make talking about art easier.

Cut cardboard or inner tube to make a printing surface glue to a backing, ink or paint and then print. Make several designs across the page.

Pieces of Styrofoam are good for cutting and printing.

Depth in art is an impression.

Depth can be shown by overlapping by size differences, by shading or by perspective.

Make some drawings to show a difference in size by what you choose to show.

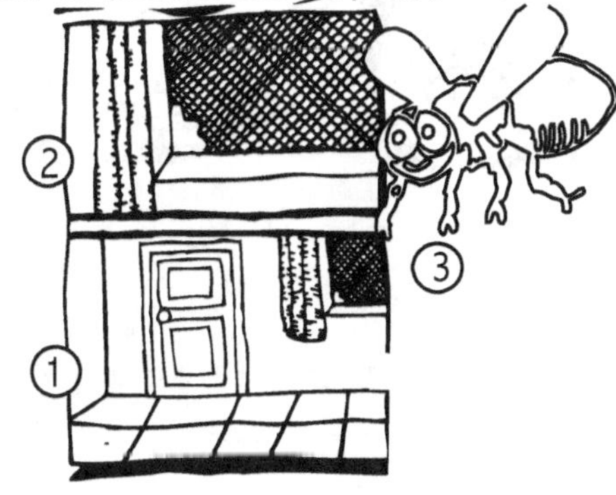

Art Alive

Make a "carp" flag. Use tissue paper to make a hollow tube so the wind can blow through it. Look at fish or pictures of fish to see how the scales, fins and gills go. Carp flags are used to celebrate Boy's Day in Japan.

AESTHETIC JUDGMENT: it happens all along as you ask yourself what parts you like best? Is there a special color you used? Is the balance of the design what you would like? Did it do what you wanted it to do?

Art Alive

SEPTEMBER IS A GOOD MONTH FOR WORKING WITH LINE!

Line is one of the elements of art. It has emotional qualities as well as descriptive qualities and it is a part of the necessary vocabulary of art.

Draw a shape. Have someone draw inside your shape something you suggest. Don't make your shape too complicated.

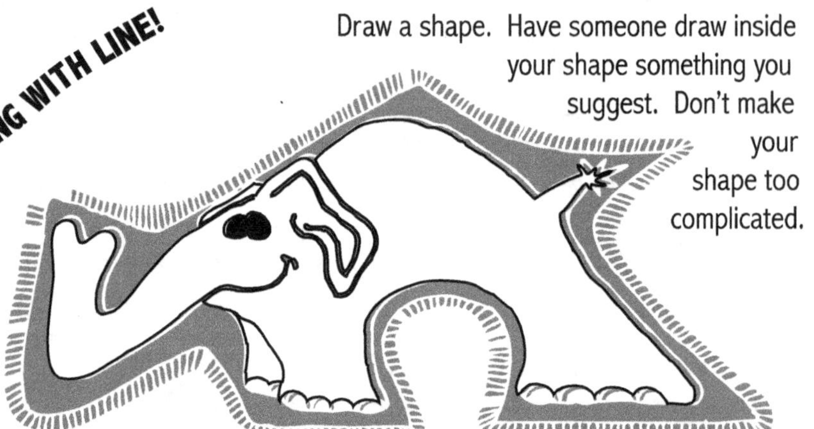

Make a design with curvy lines across a paper. Should reach from side to side. When you like it, cut it into 9 equal sectiions. Put it back together in another way. When you are happy with that, paste your new design on another piece of paper.

VARIATIONS ON ONE THEME (BICYCLE)

Take a look at bicycles or at pictures of bicycles find a section you like and draw that section. Find another section and do it again. Find another section and do it one more time. Do you begin to see a quality of line in your work?

The secret of drawing is to see something with new eyes! Find your new eyes for seeing by trying to look at the world in unusual ways... upside down, or sideways. If this means taking the world apart, then do it.

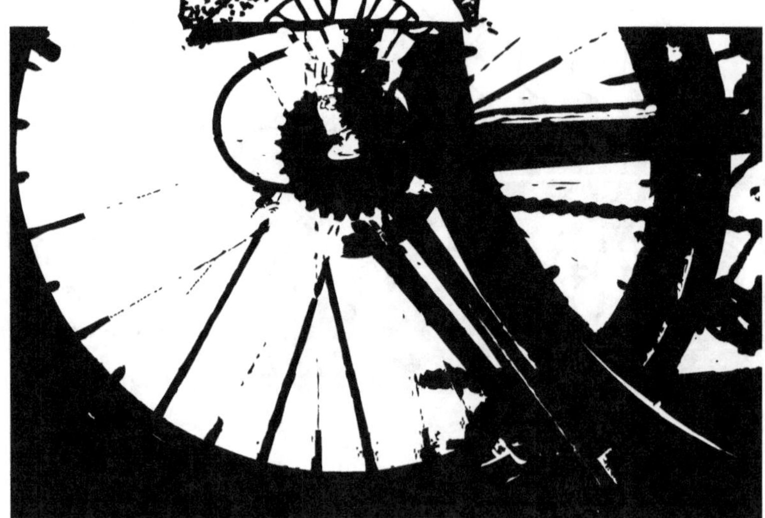

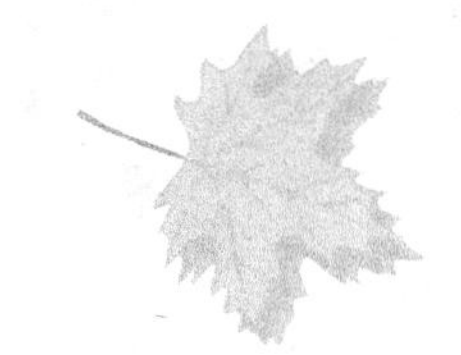

Using tempera paints, paint a continuous wavy line from one side of the paper to the other side. Follow along the first line with other lines. Then add to the rhythm of your painting with an emphasis on one of the lines. Let your lines have fun together. Stop when you like what you've done.

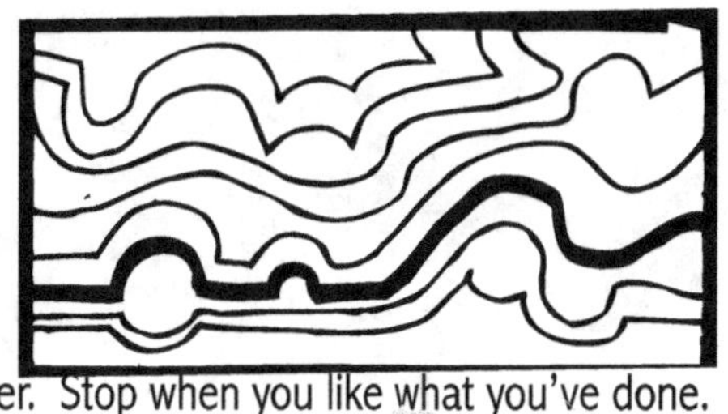

Hang out with the five basic elements all year!

Line

Shape

Color

SPACE

Texture

September

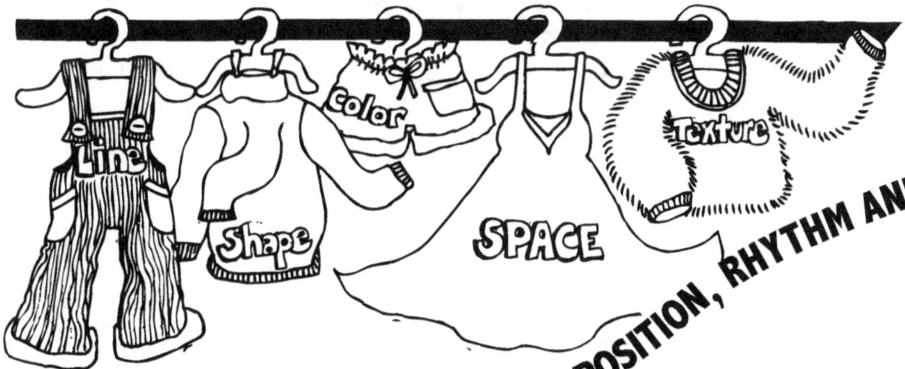

USE THE PRINCIPLES OF: EMPHASIS, OPPOSITION, RHYTHM AND BALANCE.

Use sheets of Styrofoam from meat trays.

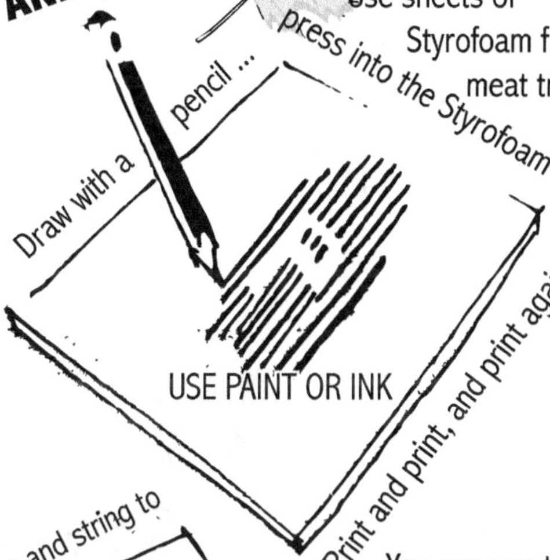

Draw with a pencil ... press into the Styrofoam tray.

USE PAINT OR INK

Print and print, and print again

Will-hold glue and cardboard.

Build sculptures from cut pieces of cardboard.

Make hand puppets out of paper bags. For the mouth fold a circle and half glue to the bottom of the bag.

Use white glue and string to

You can use this as a printing surface or as it is colored in for a design.

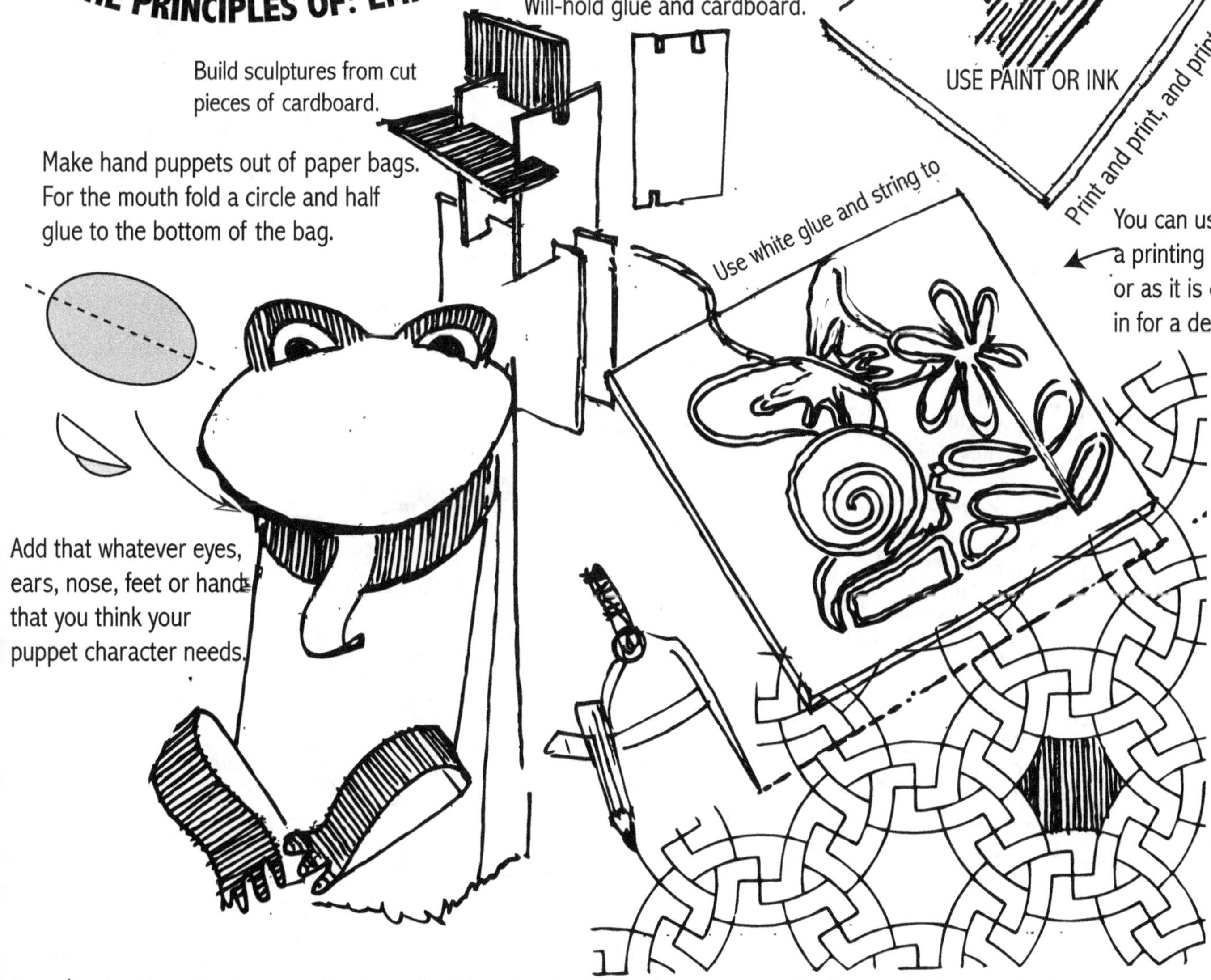

Add that whatever eyes, ears, nose, feet or hands that you think your puppet character needs.

Look at the designs of the Middle East for the wonderful repetition of elements.

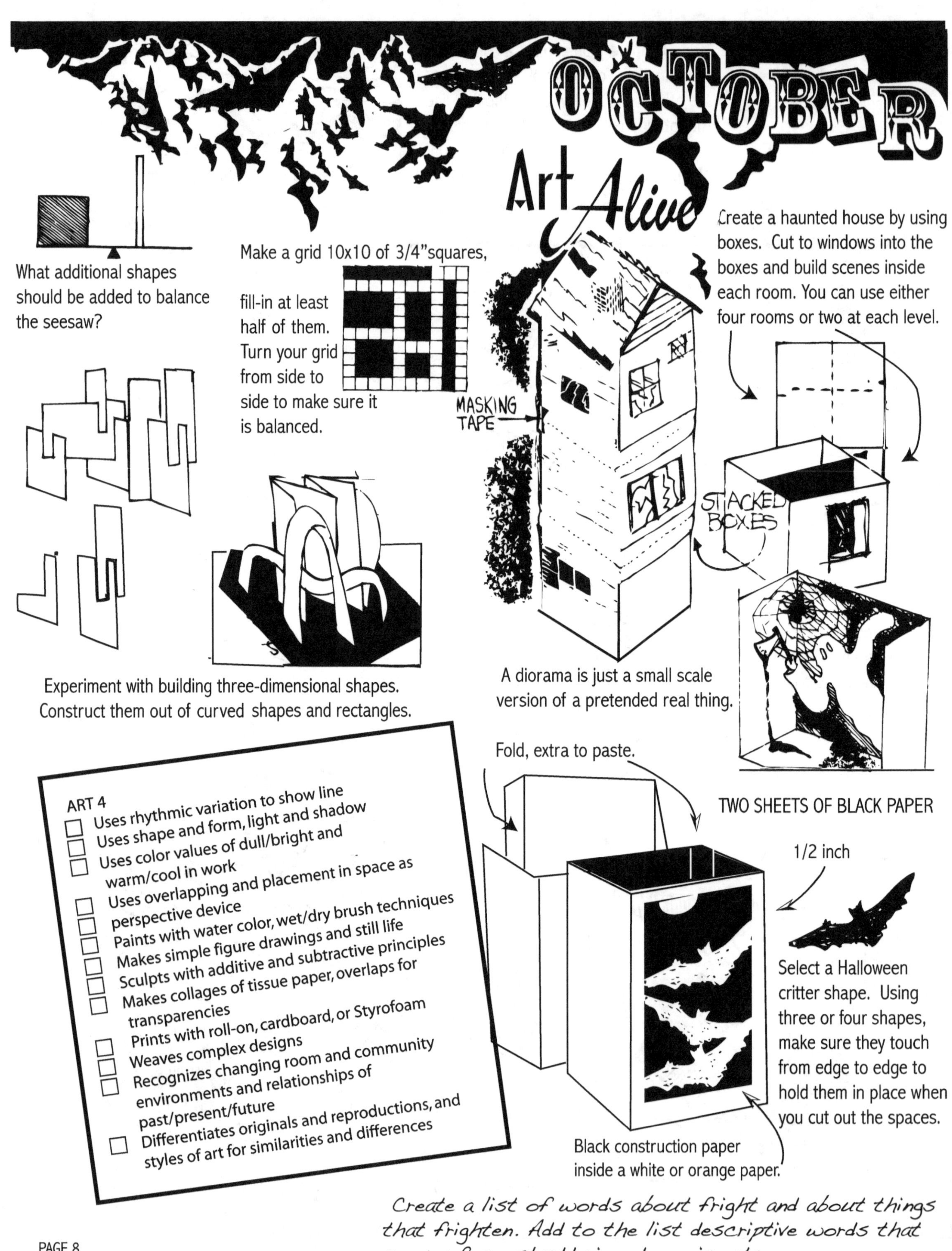
OCTOBER
Art Alive
What additional shapes should be added to balance the seesaw?
Make a grid 10x10 of 3/4"squares, fill-in at least half of them. Turn your grid from side to side to make sure it is balanced.
MASKING TAPE
Create a haunted house by using boxes. Cut to windows into the boxes and build scenes inside each room. You can use either four rooms or two at each level.
STACKED BOXES
Experiment with building three-dimensional shapes. Construct them out of curved shapes and rectangles.
A diorama is just a small scale version of a pretended real thing.
Fold, extra to paste.
TWO SHEETS OF BLACK PAPER
1/2 inch
Select a Halloween critter shape. Using three or four shapes, make sure they touch from edge to edge to hold them in place when you cut out the spaces.
Black construction paper inside a white or orange paper.
ART 4
☐ Uses rhythmic variation to show line
☐ Uses shape and form, light and shadow
☐ Uses color values of dull/bright and warm/cool in work
☐ Uses overlapping and placement in space as perspective device
☐ Paints with water color, wet/dry brush techniques
☐ Makes simple figure drawings and still life
☐ Sculpts with additive and subtractive principles
☐ Makes collages of tissue paper, overlaps for transparencies
☐ Prints with roll-on, cardboard, or Styrofoam
☐ Weaves complex designs
☐ Recognizes changing room and community environments and relationships of past/present/future
☐ Differentiates originals and reproductions, and styles of art for similarities and differences
Create a list of words about fright and about things that frighten. Add to the list descriptive words that convey fear...shuddering, demonic, etc.

Art Alive

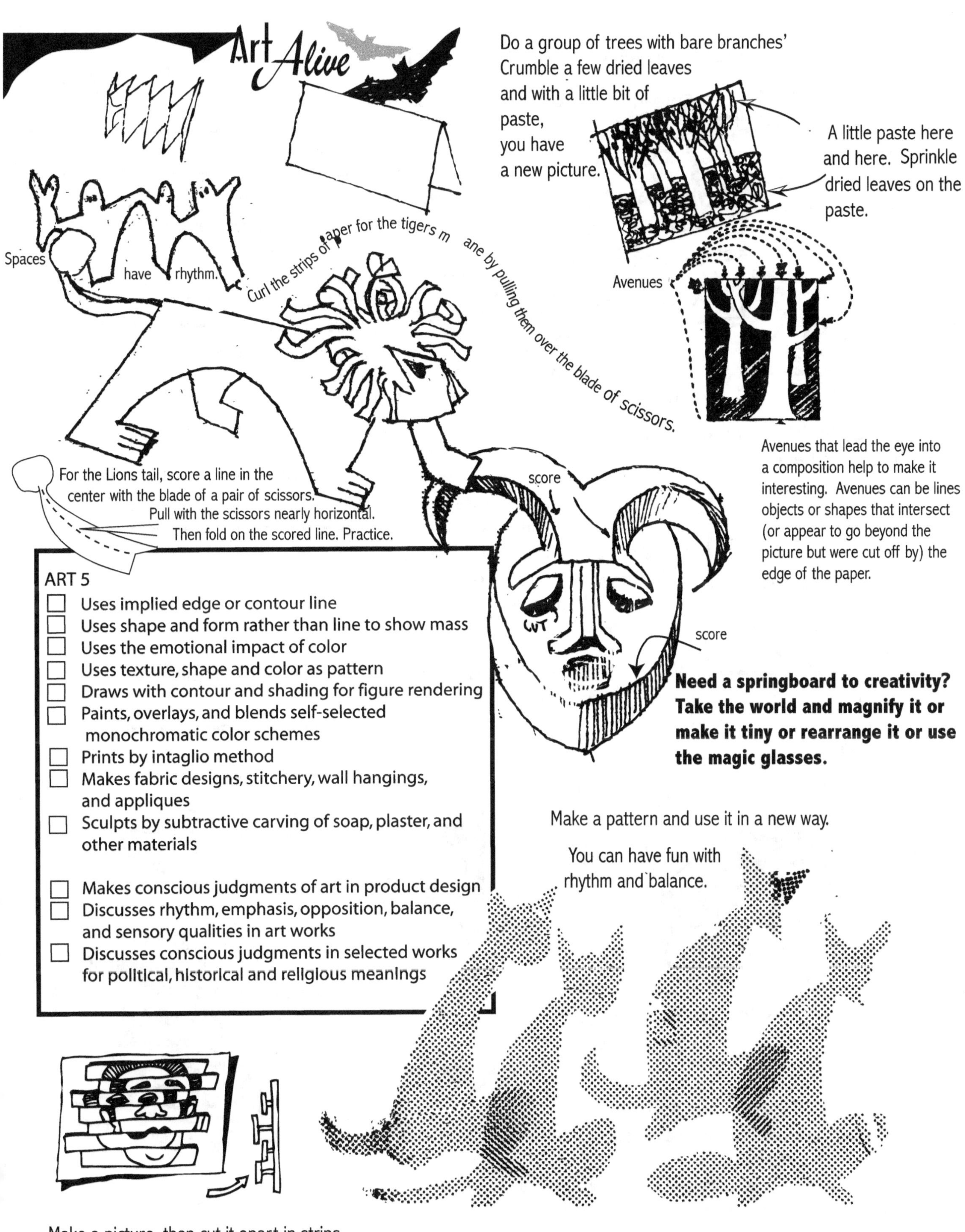

Do a group of trees with bare branches' Crumble a few dried leaves and with a little bit of paste, you have a new picture.

A little paste here and here. Sprinkle dried leaves on the paste.

Avenues that lead the eye into a composition help to make it interesting. Avenues can be lines objects or shapes that intersect (or appear to go beyond the picture but were cut off by) the edge of the paper.

For the Lions tail, score a line in the center with the blade of a pair of scissors. Pull with the scissors nearly horizontal. Then fold on the scored line. Practice.

ART 5

- ☐ Uses implied edge or contour line
- ☐ Uses shape and form rather than line to show mass
- ☐ Uses the emotional impact of color
- ☐ Uses texture, shape and color as pattern
- ☐ Draws with contour and shading for figure rendering
- ☐ Paints, overlays, and blends self-selected monochromatic color schemes
- ☐ Prints by intaglio method
- ☐ Makes fabric designs, stitchery, wall hangings, and appliques
- ☐ Sculpts by subtractive carving of soap, plaster, and other materials
- ☐ Makes conscious judgments of art in product design
- ☐ Discusses rhythm, emphasis, opposition, balance, and sensory qualities in art works
- ☐ Discusses conscious judgments in selected works for political, historical and religious meanings

Need a springboard to creativity? Take the world and magnify it or make it tiny or rearrange it or use the magic glasses.

Make a pattern and use it in a new way.

You can have fun with rhythm and balance.

Make a picture, then cut it apart in strips. Glue the strips to a piece of folded paper so they are on different levels.

Wrap string around a brayer. Crisscross it several times.

Art Alive

Spread some poster paint on cardboard.

ART 6th

- ☐ uses dynamic and static line to create tension
- ☐ uses shape and form for opposition and balance
- ☐ uses color value and variations of hue for light influence
- ☐ uses light values of space for perspective
- ☐ uses tactile effects for texture
- ☐ draws with negative as well as positive shapes
- ☐ designs floor plans, posters, and covers
- ☐ prints with two or more colors
- ☐ weaves natural materials
- ☐ makes conscious judgments of art as quality of life
- ☐ discusses contributions of selected artists and periods

Make sure it's just a thin layer.

Roll the brayer lightly in the ink and then onto your paper.

You can add to the complexity of your design if you print it in the other direction also.

Use a squeeze bottle white glue and make design lines across a piece of paper. When the glue dries, paint between the raised areas.

Make your own zoo of wild animals with simple folds in a piece of paper.

Create your own design for animals.

Use old pieces of cloth and stitch a scene or design.

GROWTH: WHAT TO LOOK FOR

- ☆ a willingness to experiment with changing normal shapes to make them closer to a mood or expression
- ☆ an ability to organize visual impressions into shape arrangements
- ☆ an ability to synthesize new relationships for emphasis.

Sunset is a good time to look for shapes both in the sky and on the horizon. Animated cartoons use shapes to emphasize the character and the mood.

LOOK, USE, TALK ABOUT THE BASIC ELEMENTS (COLOR, SPACE, SHAPE, TEXTURE, LINE).

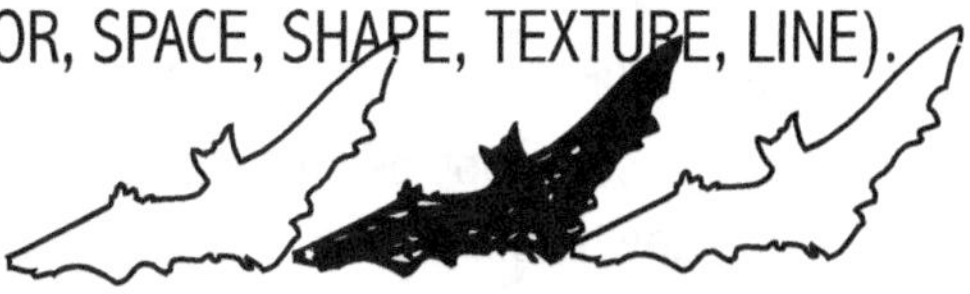

PERCEPTION — *Seeing*

Spend time looking. Use your Magic Viewer cards
What is it like? What is the important part of it?

EXPRESSION — *Doing*

What do I think is important? How can I best show it?

JUDGMENT — *Responding*

Did my drawing or design do what I wanted?
Does it look good? What parts do I like best?
Does it remind me of anything else?

Pumpkins are great things to draw. Before you cut them for jack-o'-lanterns draw them.

You can gain a nice design quality by not looking at the paper while you sketch them.

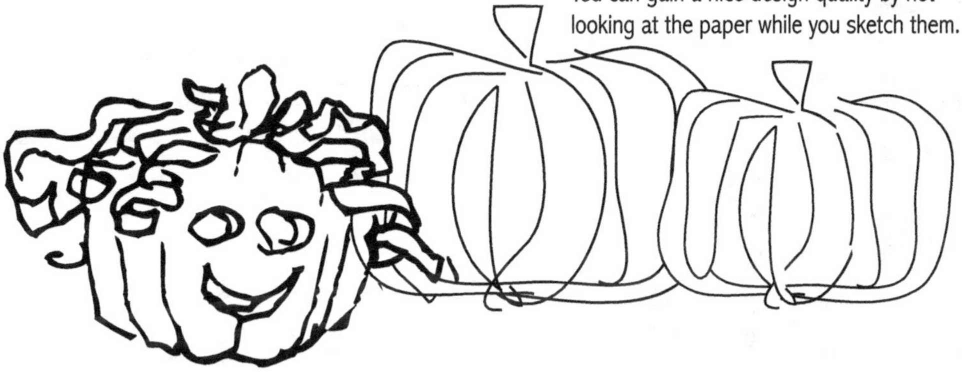

if you have a jack-o'-lantern shouldn't you have a Jill-o'-lantern.

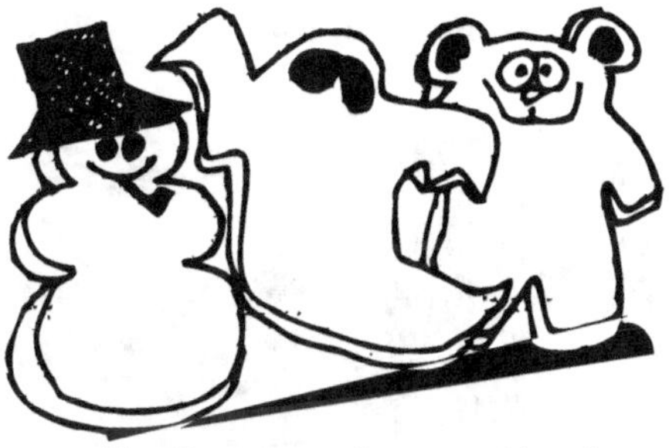

Use Styrofoam from packing for an easy way to cut shapes ...any kind of shapes that you want. Cut from a curve of the packing for a variety of shapes.

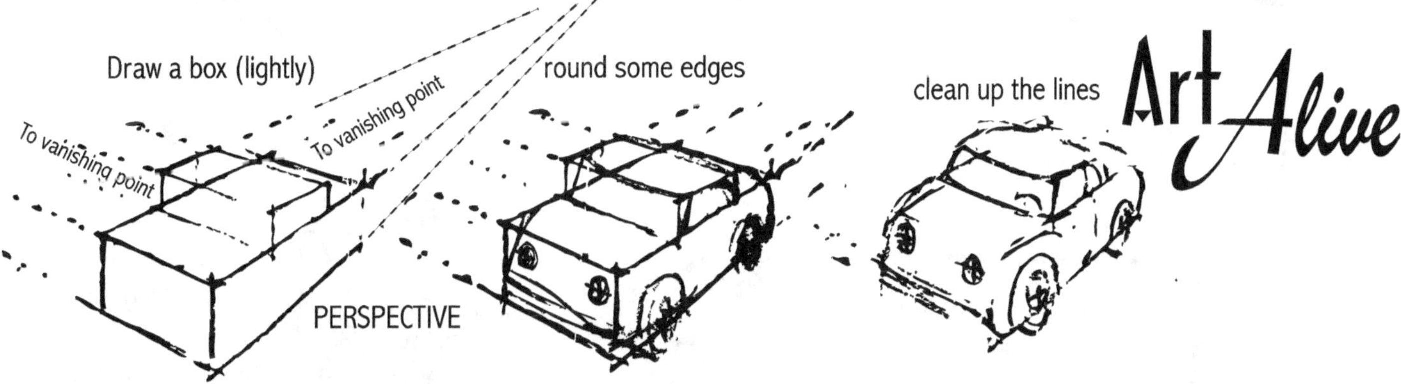

PERSPECTIVE IS ONE WAY TO SHOW SPACE, OVERLAPPING FORMS IS ANOTHER, SIZE IS ANOTHER.

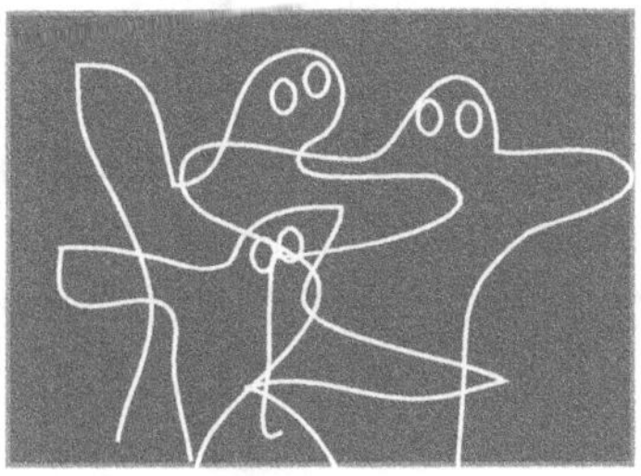

Crayon resist uses the wax of a crayon to keep thin paint or ink from the paper. Use white crayon with black or gray for free form ghosts or with colors and blue for underwater scenes... or use your imagination. Try pumpkins with orange crayon and black paint.

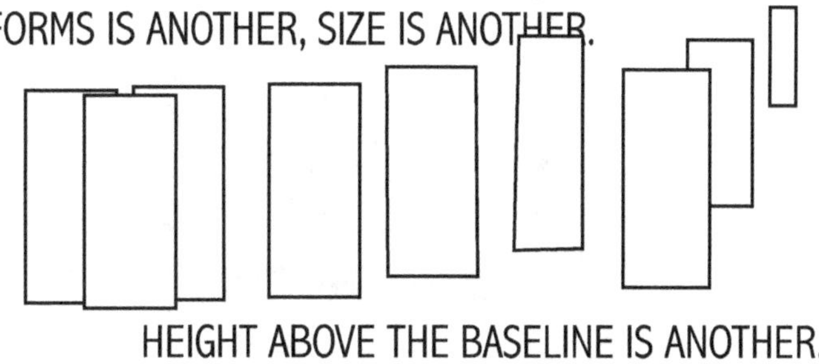

HEIGHT ABOVE THE BASELINE IS ANOTHER.

NOVEMBER

Art Alive

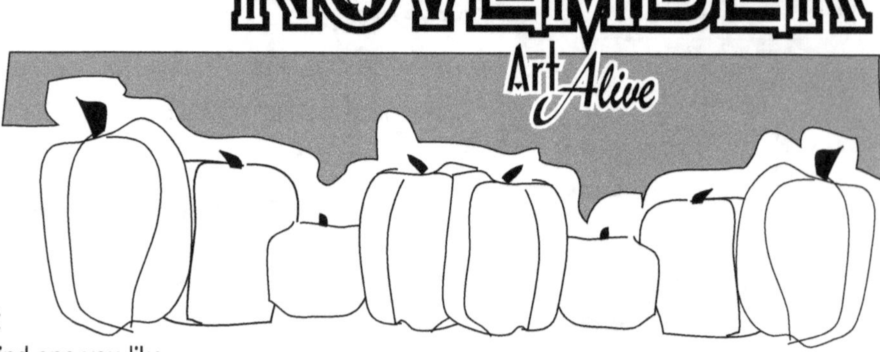

Perception

Collect some apples, make a row of apples arrange them in order of color.

Expression

Draw what you see.

Aesthetic judgment

Eat an apple.
Did you like the taste?
Draw an apple core. Does it have the feel of an eaten apple? Did you like what you drew? Draw other apples until you find one you like.

November is a time to look at trees, leaves, the sky, clothes. Find a new color that you like, then write the first thought that comes to your mind about that color.
Write another thought and then another. Make a design, or a painting, or a sculpture that shows your ideas about the color.

Use negative spaces as well as positives in your work. Have fun with your art.

Let the spaces in your artwork be as important as the lines.

Accordion folded paper.

Make popsicle stick puppets of characters in one of your readings. Make a play about the story

Have fun making your turkeys. Use your imagination.

An easy way to make Thanksgiving turkeys is with a regular grocery bag. You can add a tail with folded construction paper or with feathers cut from paper.

Use a bent coat hanger and stretch old nylons over it for the head and the neck. Tie or tape it to a paper bag.

All life is just making choices. Aesthetic judgment is the valuing of choices made in art. It is a necessary part of any activity and each move of your pencil or brush is a new choice.

DO SOME NAME DESIGNS

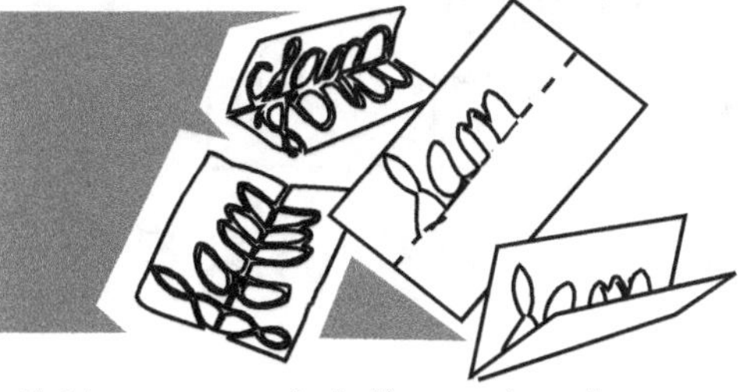

Fold your paper in half, open it and on one side write your name. Close the paper with your name on the inside. Against the window or light source trace your name through it to the other side. Color the background and open areas.

More turkey place cards.

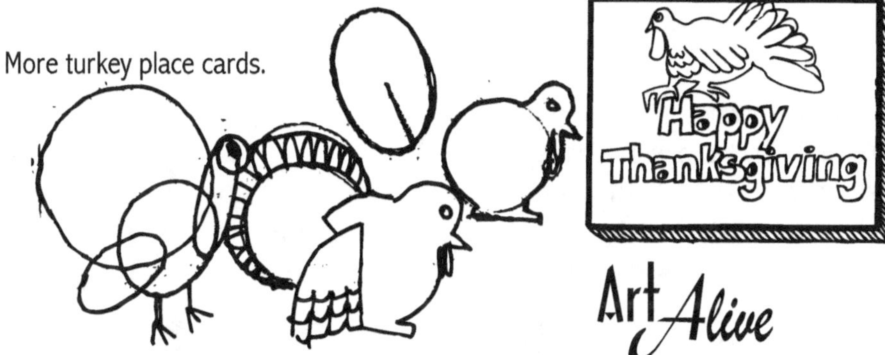

You can use this idea for other seasons of the year.

ART 6

- ☐ Uses dynamic and static line to create tension
- ☐ Uses shape and form for opposition and balance
- ☐ Uses color value and variations of hue for light influence
- ☐ Uses light values of space for perspective
- ☐ Uses tactile effects for texture
- ☐ Draws with negative as well as positive shapes
- ☐ Designs floor plans, posters, and covers
- ☐ Prints with two or more colors
- ☐ Weaves natural materials
- ☐ Makes conscious judgments of art as a quality of life
- ☐ Discusses contributions of selected artists and periods

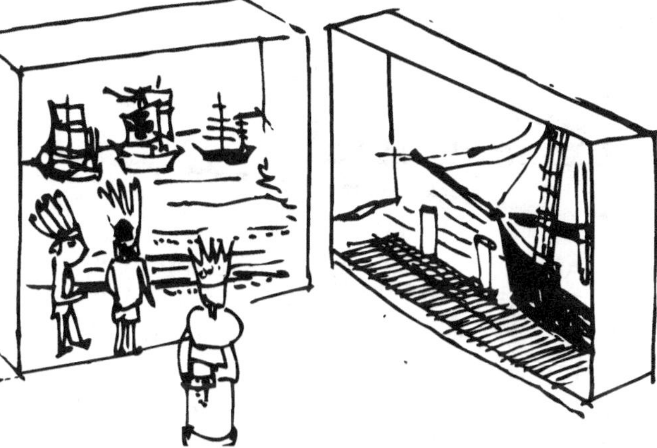

Make dioramas of what you know of Columbus's Voyage. Go back to your history books, if needs be.

GIANT PORTRAITS

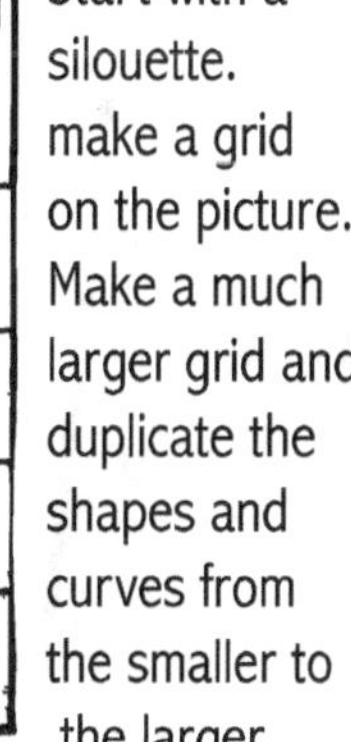

Start with a silouette. make a grid on the picture. Make a much larger grid and duplicate the shapes and curves from the smaller to the larger.

Trace action figures of yourself on butcher paper. Cut them out and overlap them on a larger paper.

Do a line drawing of yourself! Looking in the mirror.

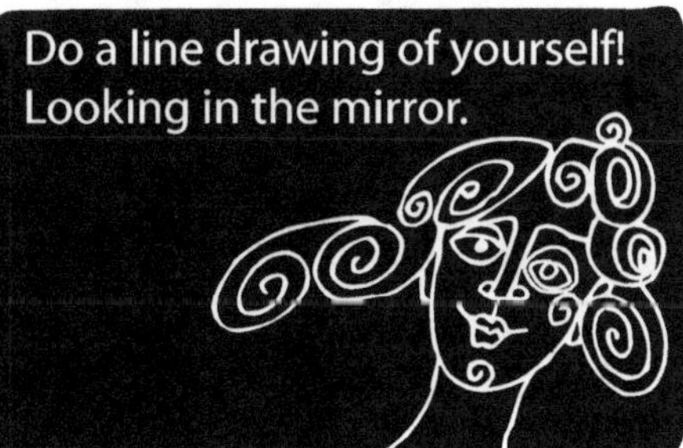

Draw some things that make lines

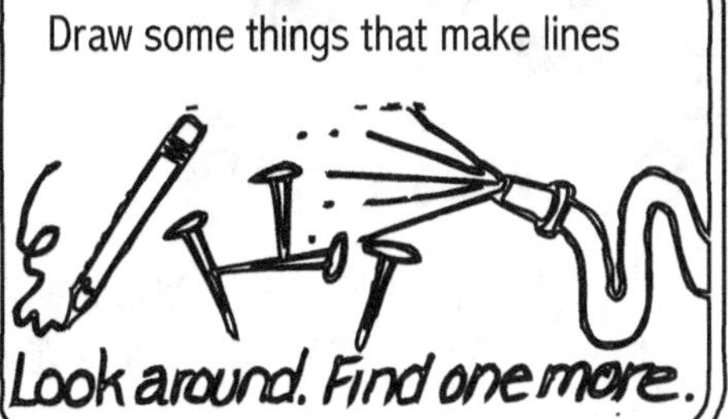

Look around. Find one more.

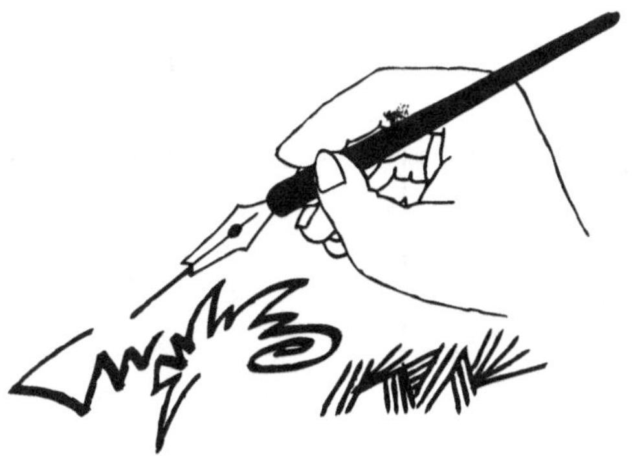

If you've nothing to do, make a dimensional sculpture on scraps of paper.

Size alone is nothing unless it is compared to something else.

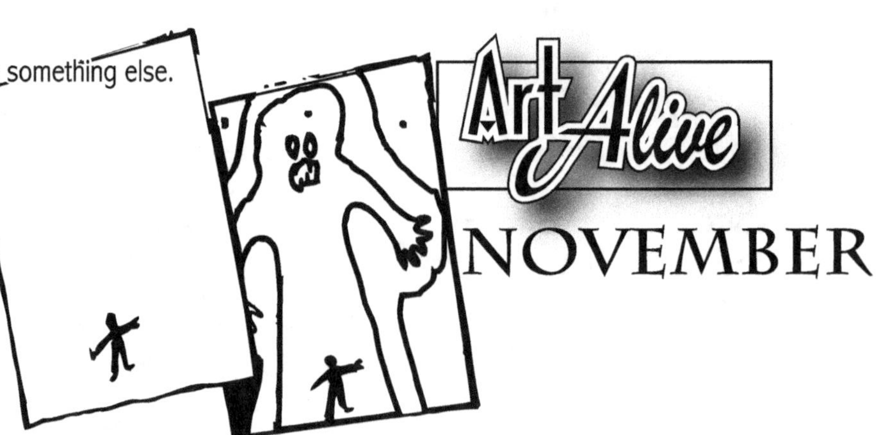

NOVEMBER

Cut some thin Styrofoam into shapes that you like. They can be realistic shapes or just shapes. Draw on them with a pencil to make textural indentations.

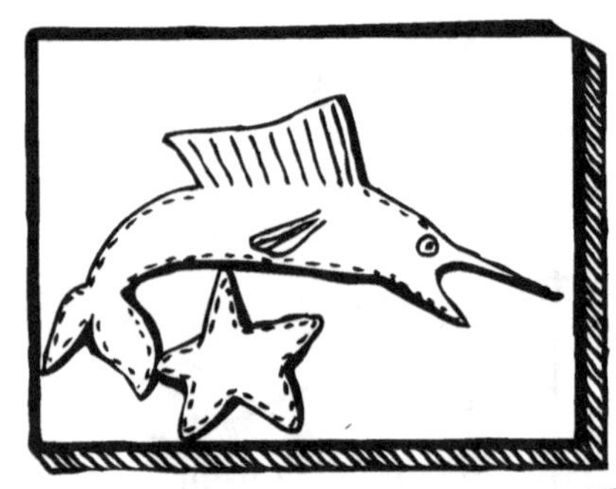

Explore in some drawings the way to compare objects in a picture.

Use a plastic bottle and with a razor knife. Be very careful!

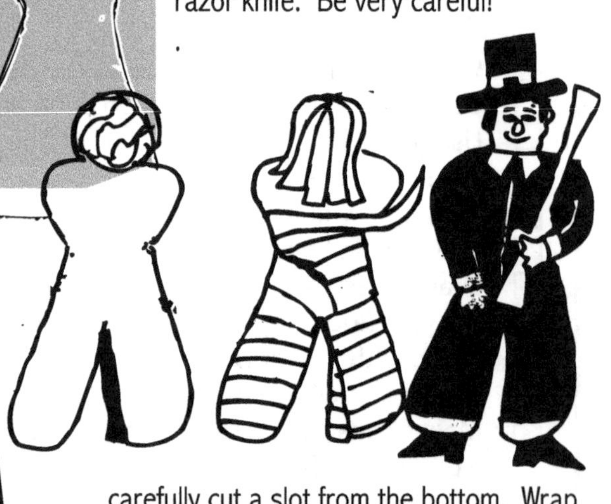

carefully cut a slot from the bottom. Wrap with strips of newspaper that have been wet by white glue or wallpaper paste. Paint and add the hat and gun. You can make Mrs.. Pilgrim also.

ART 4

- ☐ Uses rhythmic variation to show line
- ☐ Uses shape and form, light and shadow
- ☐ Uses color values of dull/bright and warm/cool in work
- ☐ Uses overlapping and placement in space as perspective device
- ☐ Paints with water color, wet/dry brush techniques
- ☐ Makes simple figure drawings and still life
- ☐ Sculpts with additive and subtractive principles
- ☐ Makes collages of tissue paper, overlaps for transparencies
- ☐ Prints with roll-on, cardboard, or Styrofoam
- ☐ Weaves complex designs
- ☐ Recognizes changing room and community environments and relationships of past/present/future
- ☐ Differentiates originals and reproductions, and styles of art for similarities and differences

Make shapes showing verb tenses or adjectives.

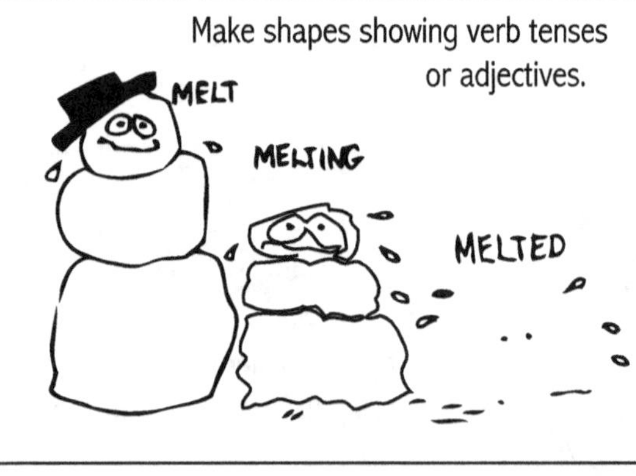

ACCORDION FOLD PAPER

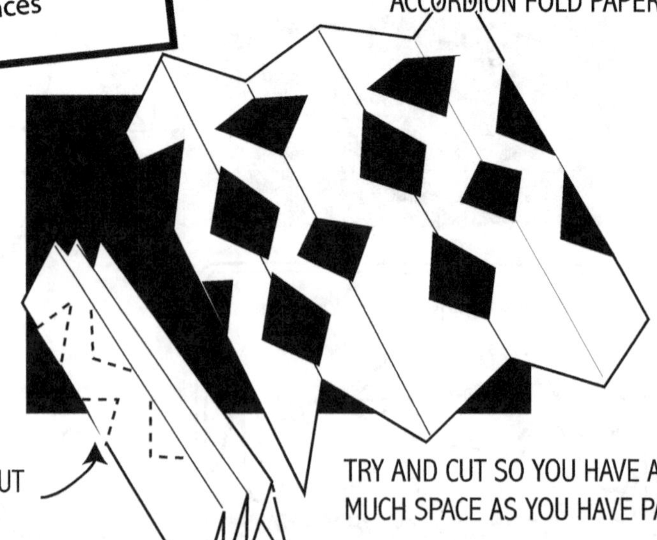

TRY AND CUT SO YOU HAVE AS MUCH SPACE AS YOU HAVE PAPER.

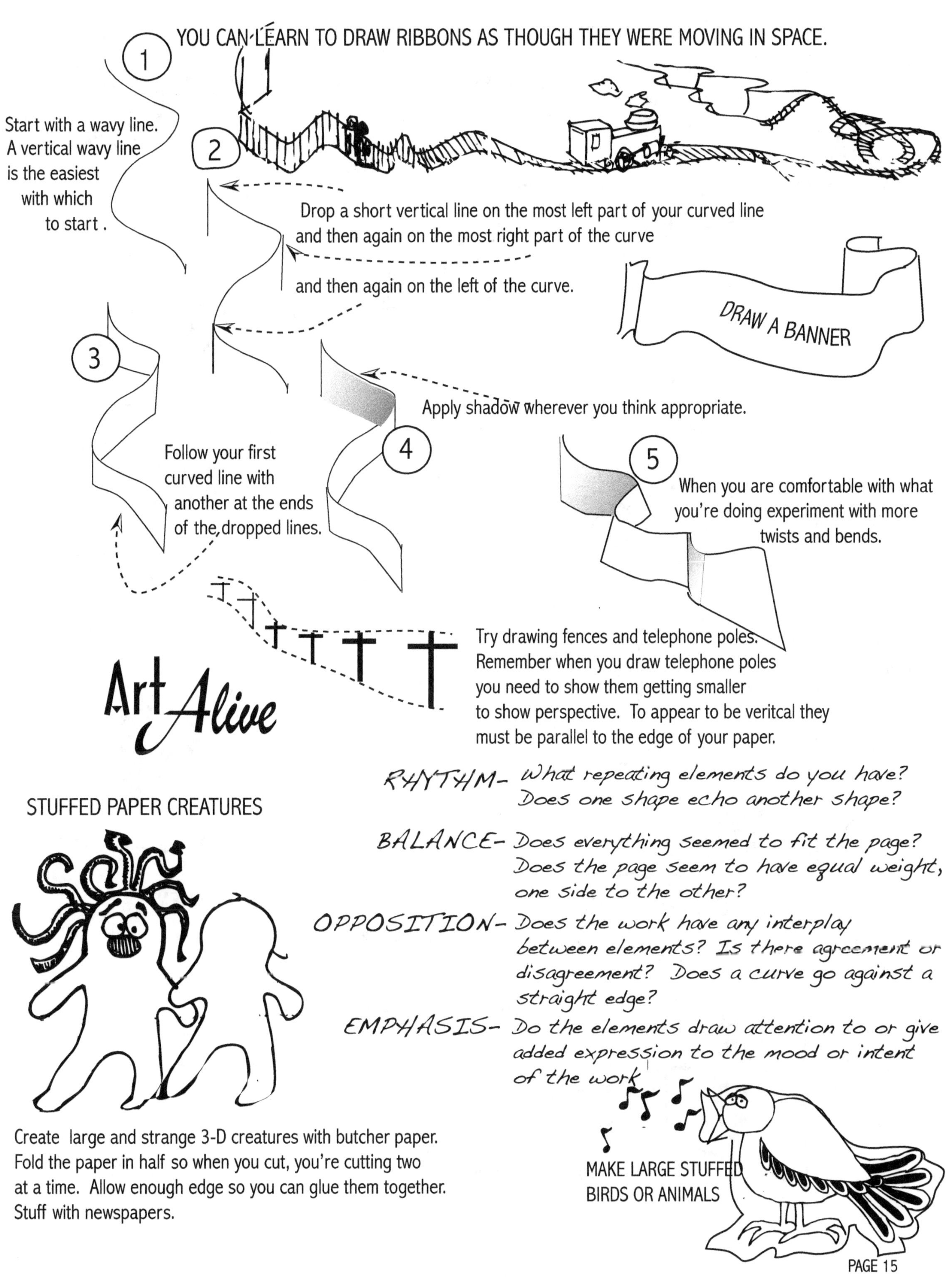
YOU CAN LEARN TO DRAW RIBBONS AS THOUGH THEY WERE MOVING IN SPACE.
1
Start with a wavy line. A vertical wavy line is the easiest with which to start .
2
Drop a short vertical line on the most left part of your curved line and then again on the most right part of the curve
and then again on the left of the curve.
DRAW A BANNER
3
Apply shadow wherever you think appropriate.
Follow your first curved line with another at the ends of the dropped lines.
4
5
When you are comfortable with what you're doing experiment with more twists and bends.
Try drawing fences and telephone poles. Remember when you draw telephone poles you need to show them getting smaller to show perspective. To appear to be veritcal they must be parallel to the edge of your paper.
Art Alive
RHYTHM- What repeating elements do you have? Does one shape echo another shape?
STUFFED PAPER CREATURES
BALANCE- Does everything seemed to fit the page? Does the page seem to have equal weight, one side to the other?
OPPOSITION- Does the work have any interplay between elements? Is there agreement or disagreement? Does a curve go against a straight edge?
EMPHASIS- Do the elements draw attention to or give added expression to the mood or intent of the work
Create large and strange 3-D creatures with butcher paper. Fold the paper in half so when you cut, you're cutting two at a time. Allow enough edge so you can glue them together. Stuff with newspapers.
MAKE LARGE STUFFED BIRDS OR ANIMALS

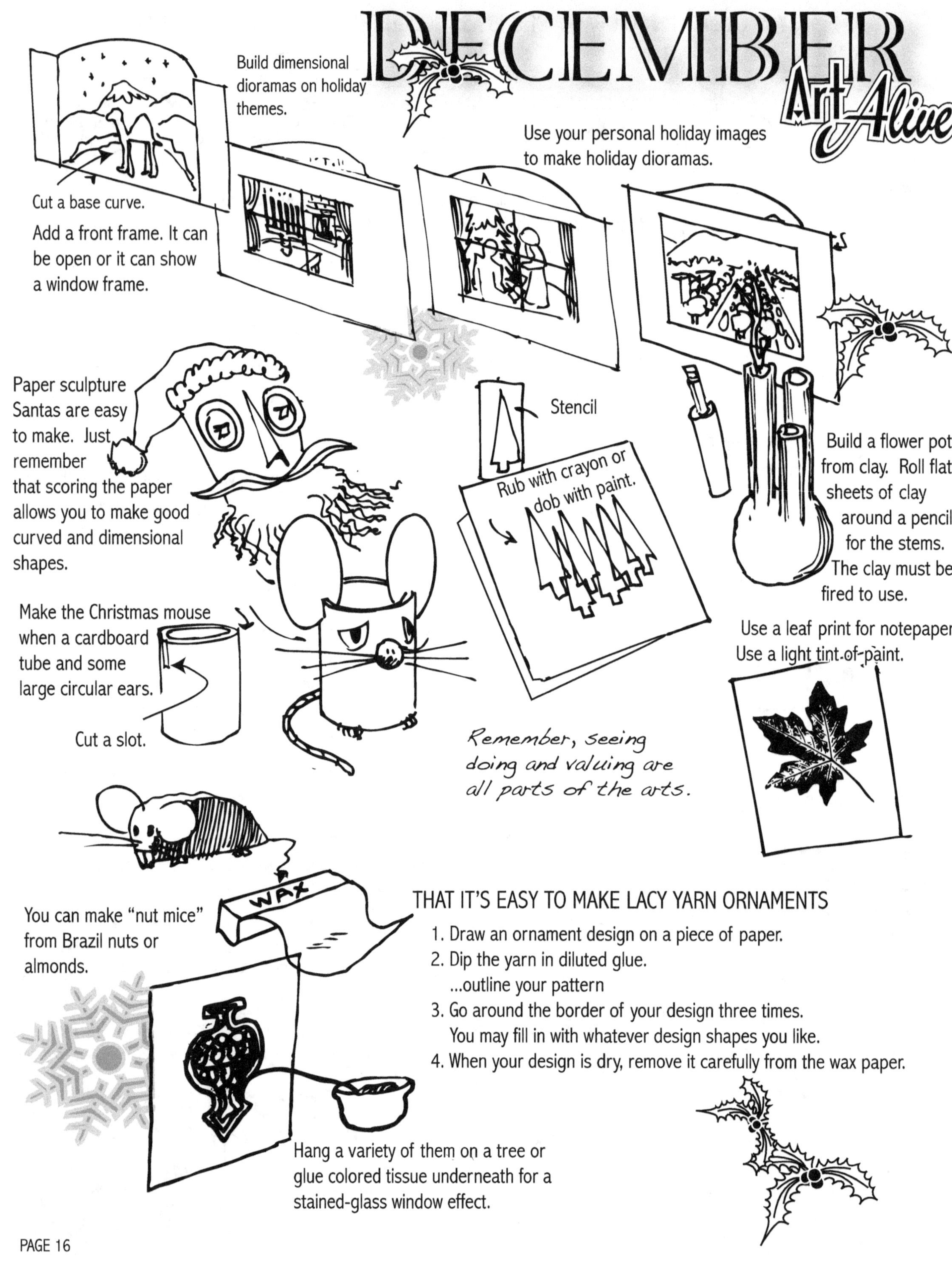
DECEMBER
Art Alive
Build dimensional dioramas on holiday themes.
Use your personal holiday images to make holiday dioramas.
Cut a base curve.
Add a front frame. It can be open or it can show a window frame.
Paper sculpture Santas are easy to make. Just remember that scoring the paper allows you to make good curved and dimensional shapes.
Stencil
Rub with crayon or dob with paint.
Build a flower pot from clay. Roll flat sheets of clay around a pencil for the stems. The clay must be fired to use.
Make the Christmas mouse when a cardboard tube and some large circular ears.
Cut a slot.
Use a leaf print for notepaper. Use a light tint of paint.
Remember, seeing doing and valuing are all parts of the arts.
You can make "nut mice" from Brazil nuts or almonds.
WAX
THAT IT'S EASY TO MAKE LACY YARN ORNAMENTS
1. Draw an ornament design on a piece of paper.
2. Dip the yarn in diluted glue.
...outline your pattern
3. Go around the border of your design three times.
You may fill in with whatever design shapes you like.
4. When your design is dry, remove it carefully from the wax paper.
Hang a variety of them on a tree or glue colored tissue underneath for a stained-glass window effect.

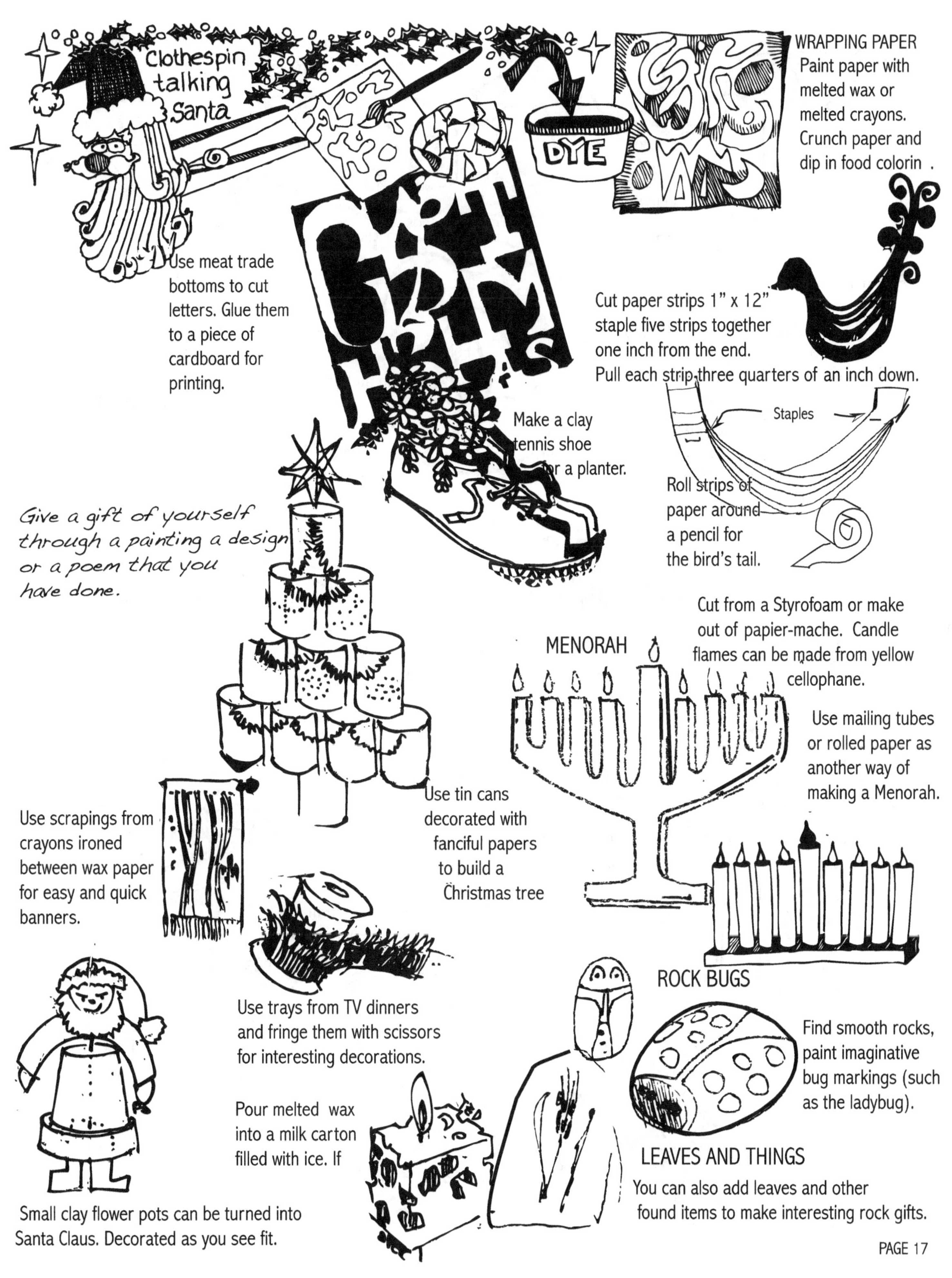
Clothespin talking Santa
DYE
WRAPPING PAPER
Paint paper with melted wax or melted crayons. Crunch paper and dip in food colorin .
Use meat trade bottoms to cut letters. Glue them to a piece of cardboard for printing.
Cut paper strips 1" x 12" staple five strips together one inch from the end.
Pull each strip three quarters of an inch down.
Staples
Make a clay tennis shoe for a planter.
Roll strips of paper around a pencil for the bird's tail.
Give a gift of yourself through a painting a design or a poem that you have done.
Cut from a Styrofoam or make out of papier-mache. Candle flames can be made from yellow cellophane.
MENORAH
Use mailing tubes or rolled paper as another way of making a Menorah.
Use tin cans decorated with fanciful papers to build a Christmas tree
Use scrapings from crayons ironed between wax paper for easy and quick banners.
ROCK BUGS
Use trays from TV dinners and fringe them with scissors for interesting decorations.
Find smooth rocks, paint imaginative bug markings (such as the ladybug).
Pour melted wax into a milk carton filled with ice. If
LEAVES AND THINGS
You can also add leaves and other found items to make interesting rock gifts.
Small clay flower pots can be turned into Santa Claus. Decorated as you see fit.

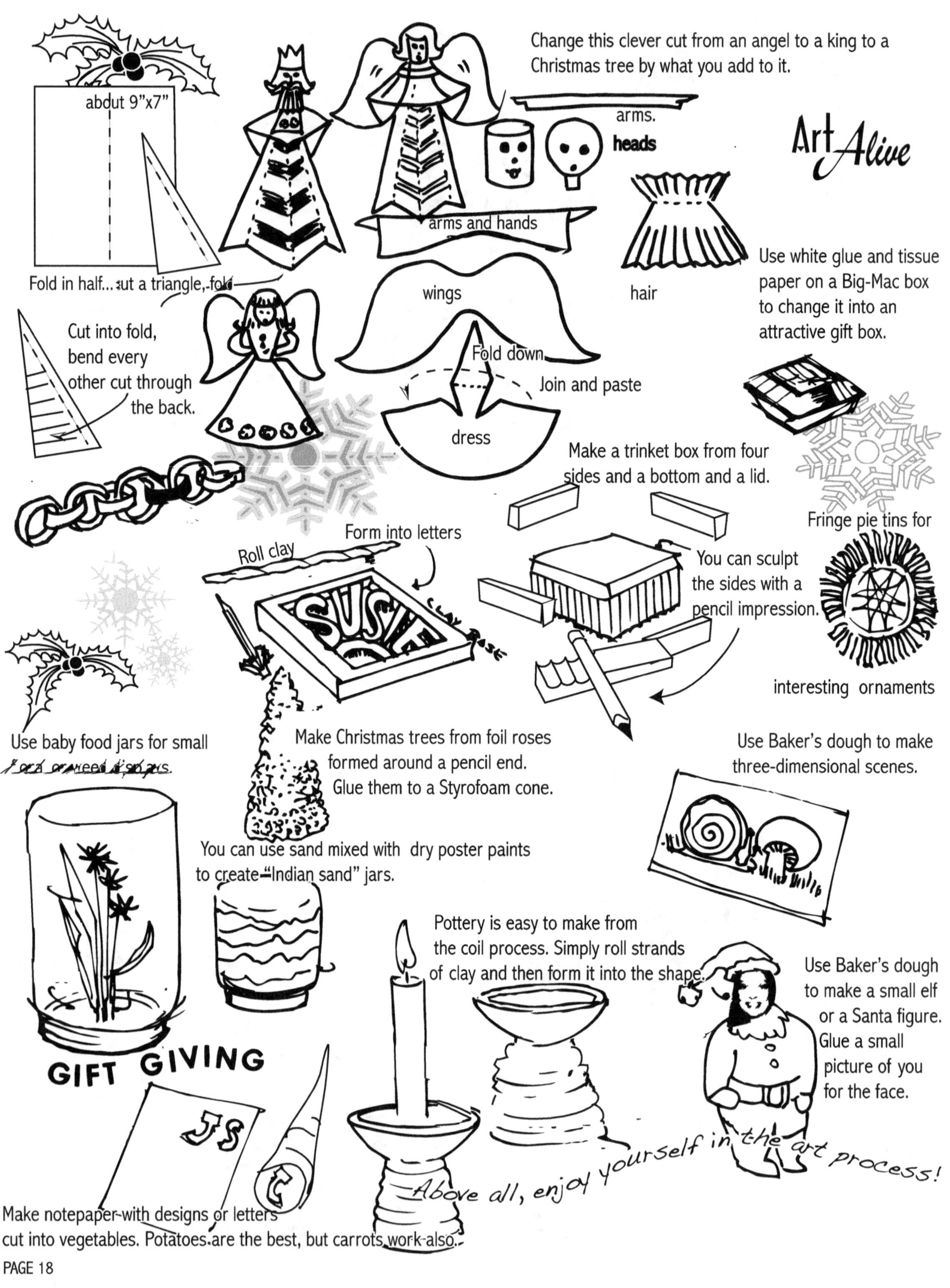
Change this clever cut from an angel to a king to a Christmas tree by what you add to it.
Art Alive
about 9"x7"
arms.
heads
arms and hands
hair
Use white glue and tissue paper on a Big-Mac box to change it into an attractive gift box.
Fold in half... cut a triangle, fold
wings
Cut into fold, bend every other cut through the back.
Fold down
Join and paste
dress
Make a trinket box from four sides and a bottom and a lid.
Fringe pie tins for
Form into letters
Roll clay
SUSIE
CLAY BASE
You can sculpt the sides with a pencil impression.
interesting ornaments
Use baby food jars for small
Make Christmas trees from foil roses formed around a pencil end. Glue them to a Styrofoam cone.
Use Baker's dough to make three-dimensional scenes.
You can use sand mixed with dry poster paints to create "Indian sand" jars.
Pottery is easy to make from the coil process. Simply roll strands of clay and then form it into the shape.
Use Baker's dough to make a small elf or a Santa figure. Glue a small picture of you for the face.
GIFT GIVING
JS
Above all, enjoy yourself in the art process!
Make notepaper with designs or letters cut into vegetables. Potatoes are the best, but carrots work also.
PAGE 18

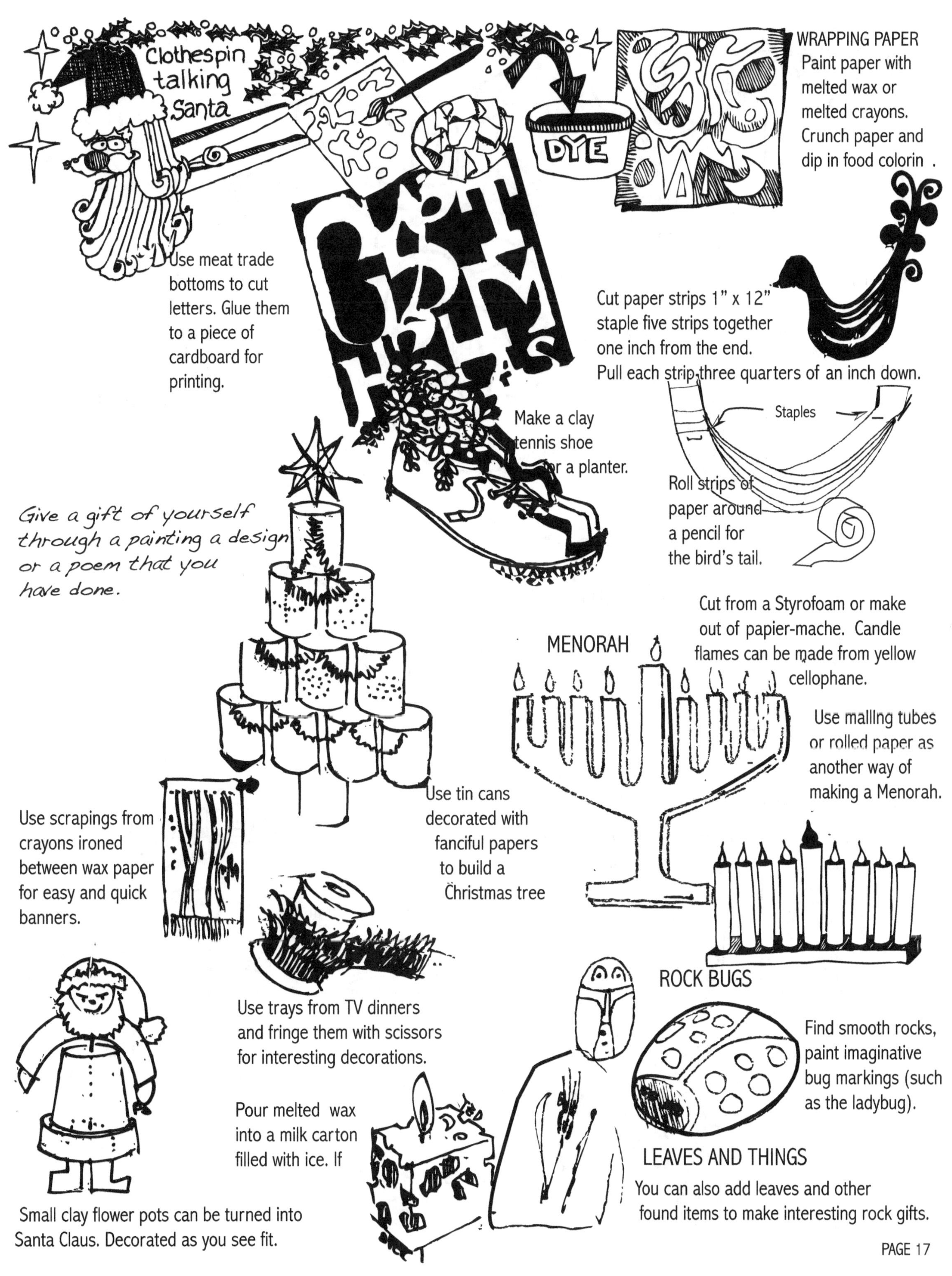

Clothespin talking Santa
WRAPPING PAPER
Paint paper with melted wax or melted crayons. Crunch paper and dip in food colorin .
DYE
Use meat trade bottoms to cut letters. Glue them to a piece of cardboard for printing.
Cut paper strips 1" x 12" staple five strips together one inch from the end. Pull each strip three quarters of an inch down.
Staples
Make a clay tennis shoe for a planter.
Roll strips of paper around a pencil for the bird's tail.
Give a gift of yourself through a painting a design or a poem that you have done.
Cut from a Styrofoam or make out of papier-mache. Candle flames can be made from yellow cellophane.
MENORAH
Use mailing tubes or rolled paper as another way of making a Menorah.
Use tin cans decorated with fanciful papers to build a Christmas tree
Use scrapings from crayons ironed between wax paper for easy and quick banners.
ROCK BUGS
Use trays from TV dinners and fringe them with scissors for interesting decorations.
Find smooth rocks, paint imaginative bug markings (such as the ladybug).
Pour melted wax into a milk carton filled with ice. If
LEAVES AND THINGS
You can also add leaves and other found items to make interesting rock gifts.
Small clay flower pots can be turned into Santa Claus. Decorated as you see fit.

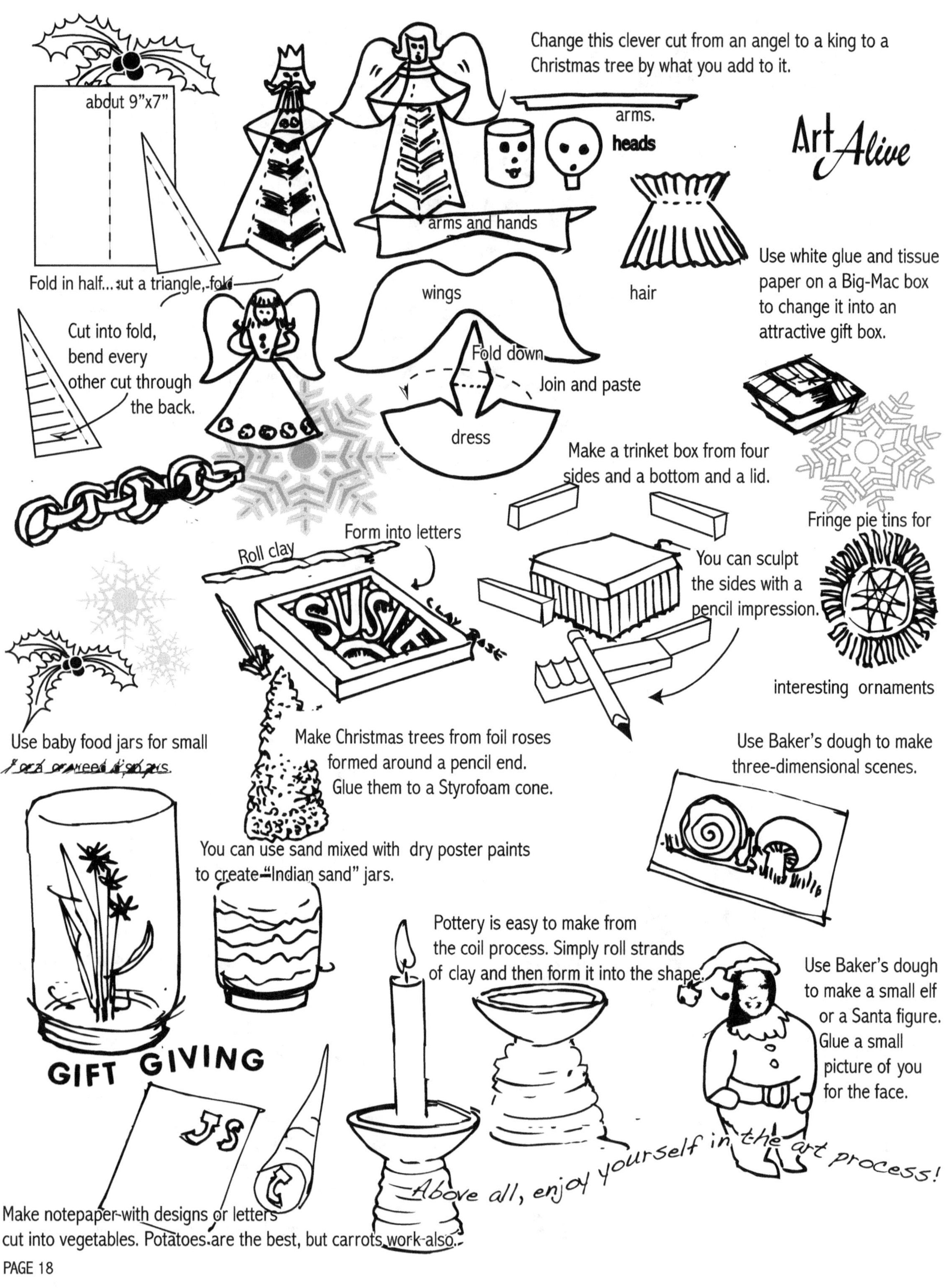

Change this clever cut from an angel to a king to a Christmas tree by what you add to it.
Art Alive
about 9"x7"
arms.
heads
arms and hands
Fold in half... cut a triangle, fold
wings
hair
Use white glue and tissue paper on a Big-Mac box to change it into an attractive gift box.
Cut into fold, bend every other cut through the back.
Fold down
Join and paste
dress
Make a trinket box from four sides and a bottom and a lid.
Fringe pie tins for
Form into letters
Roll clay
You can sculpt the sides with a pencil impression.
interesting ornaments
Use baby food jars for small
Make Christmas trees from foil roses formed around a pencil end. Glue them to a Styrofoam cone.
Use Baker's dough to make three-dimensional scenes.
You can use sand mixed with dry poster paints to create "Indian sand" jars.
Pottery is easy to make from the coil process. Simply roll strands of clay and then form it into the shape.
Use Baker's dough to make a small elf or a Santa figure. Glue a small picture of you for the face.
GIFT GIVING
Above all, enjoy yourself in the art process!
Make notepaper with designs or letters cut into vegetables. Potatoes are the best, but carrots work also.

Banners

ARE EASY TO MAKE!

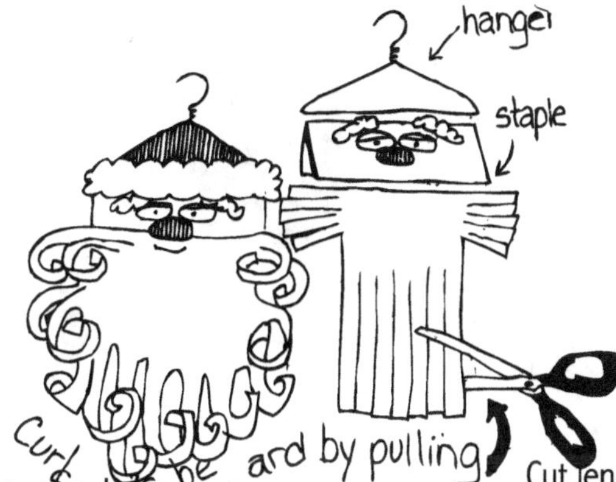

hanger

staple

Curl Santa's beard by pulling across scissors.

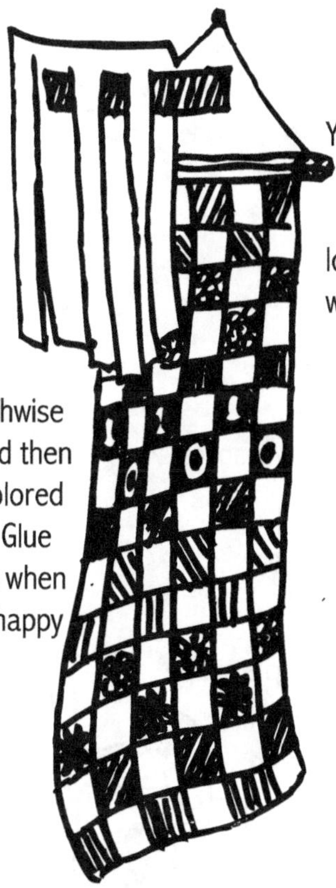

You can weave a banner out of paper. Cut strips out of butcher paper as long as you wish.

Cut lengthwise strips and then weave colored papers. Glue the ends when you are happy with it.

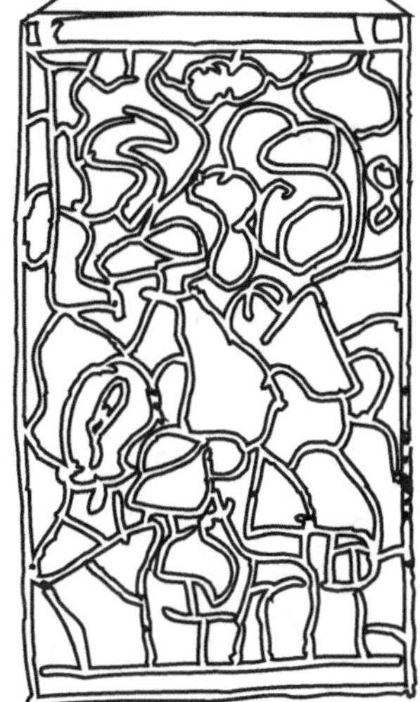

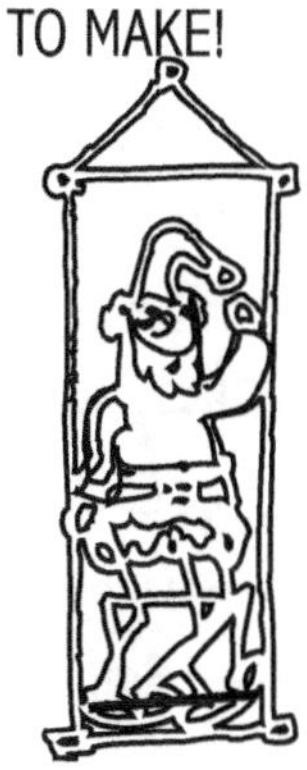

Cut out a Santa and glue it onto a piece felt.

Outline irregular shapes on butcher paper. Fill with bright colors. With light cooking oil it can become translucent.

Remember to think about opposition, balance, rhythm, an emphasis when you do your work.

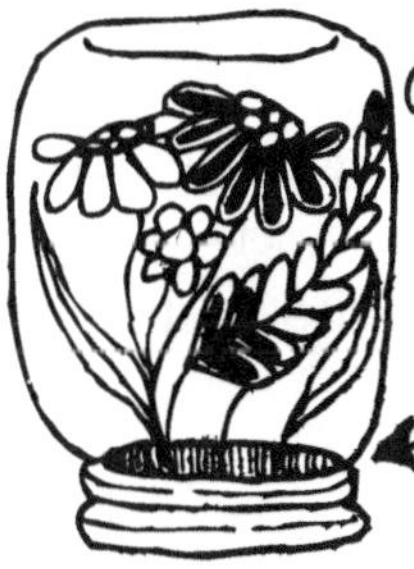

cardboard and glue

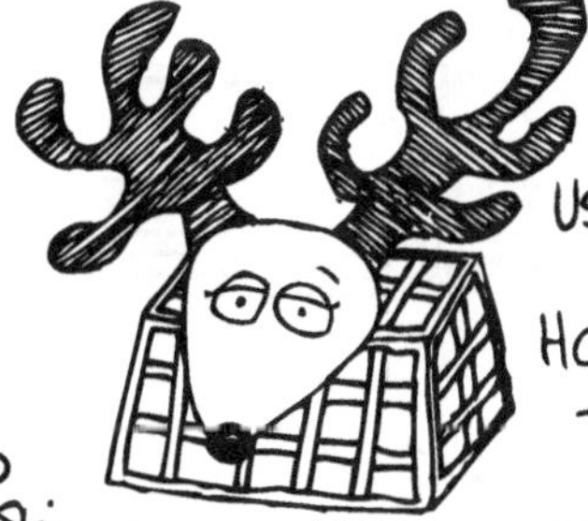

Use on your Holiday table.

Reindeer made with strawberry basket

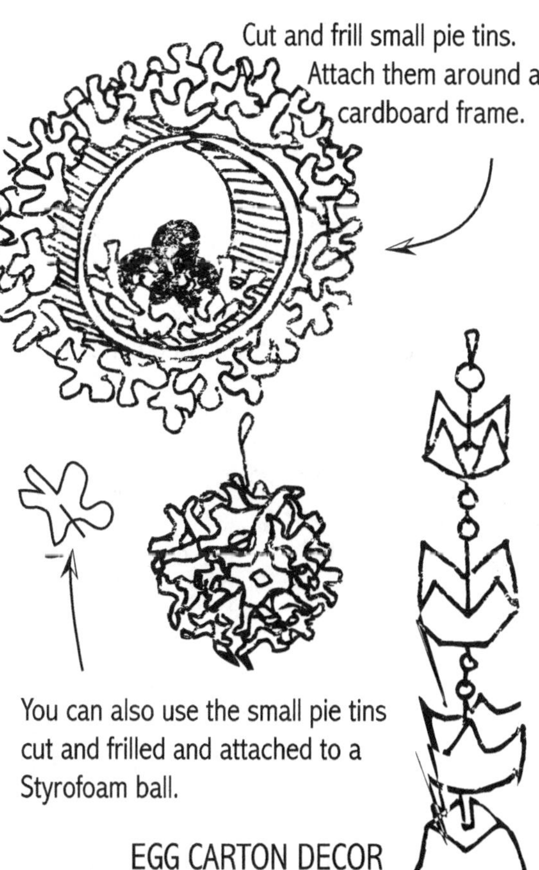

Cut and frill small pie tins. Attach them around a cardboard frame.

Roll a ball of clay about this size.

Squeeze it a bit.
Put a hole in the center.
Roll it in used coffee grounds.

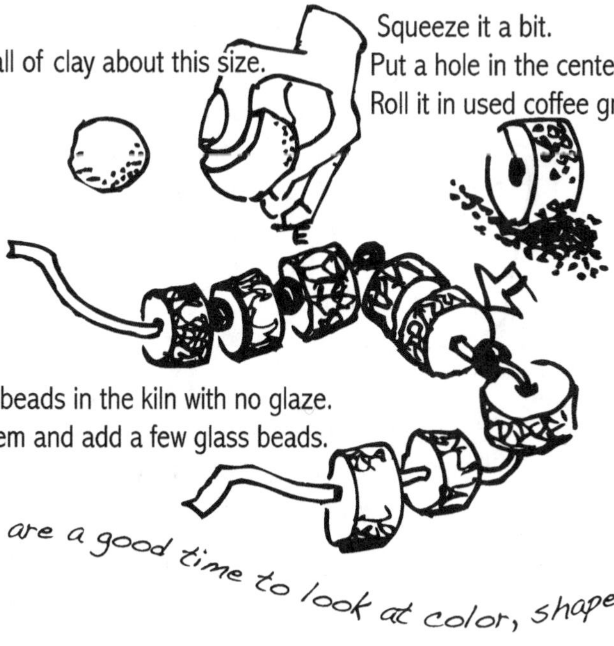

You can also use the small pie tins cut and frilled and attached to a Styrofoam ball.

Fire the beads in the kiln with no glaze.
String them and add a few glass beads.

EGG CARTON DECOR

Cut sections of egg cartons. The paint a variety of colors and connect them with string or chain.

Holidays are a good time to look at color, shapes and textures.

The Greek god Janus was noted for being able to look forward into the future and backward into the past. Use this month of January to look back at your growth and into the future for what you would like to be able to do.

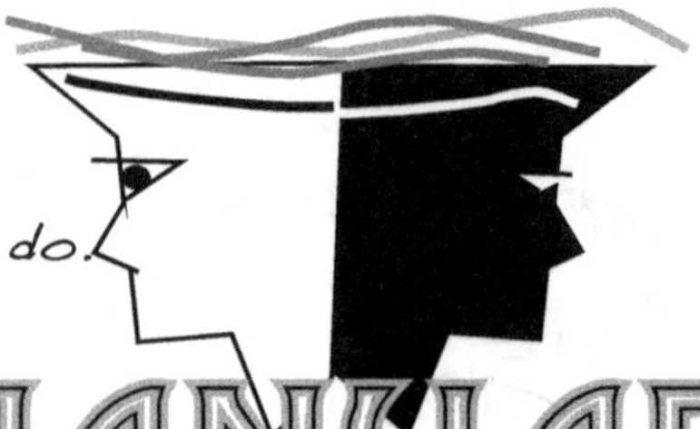

JANUARY

Art Alive

Build your vocabulary in art. Look and talk about the elements.

KNOW THE BASICS

LINE---Thick, thin, energetic, squiggly, angular.

TEXTURE--- Rough, smooth, metallic, abrasive.

SHAPE--- Circle, Square, regular, a regular, amorphous.

SPACE--- Open, closed, near, far, dimensional cramped.

COLOR--- Primary, secondary, warm, cold, kids, shades, nuances

(BE CAREFUL WITH THIS ONE)

Use three pieces of thin cardboard.

Cut a letter or simple shape with a razor knife.

Glue the letter on one of the cardboards. Glue the negative to another cardboard.

Place the two of them together and tape one edge to act as a hinge.

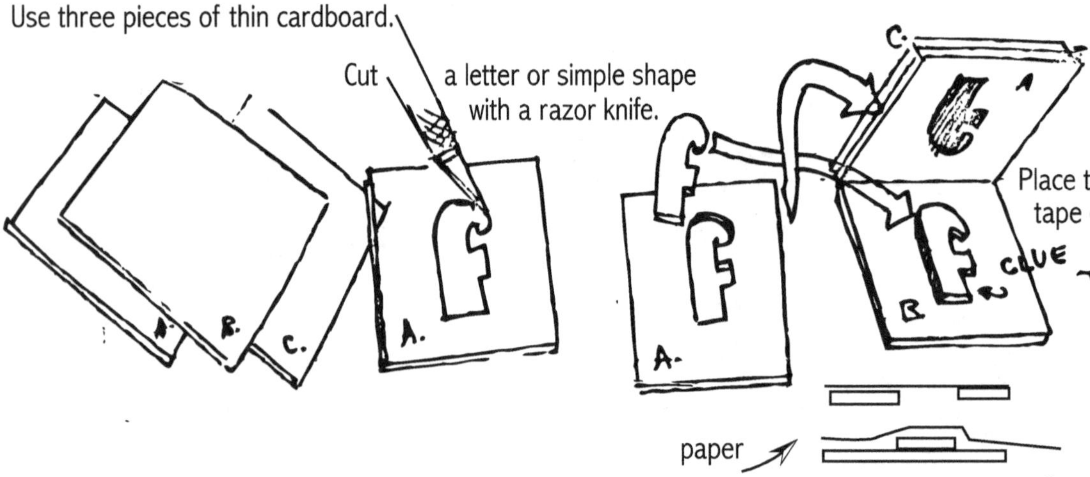

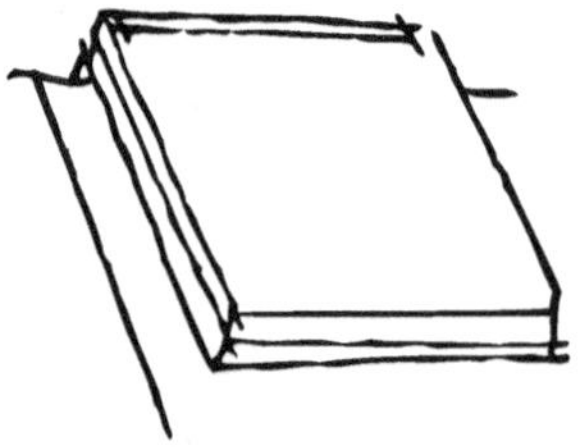

Put a piece of paper in the press and hit it with a mallet. Dampening the paper can help.

YOU CAN MAKE YOUR OWN PAPER

Build two frames 3/4" wood and about 6" square.

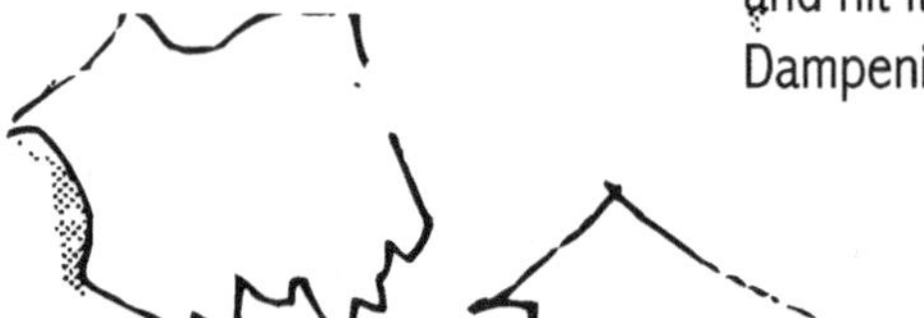

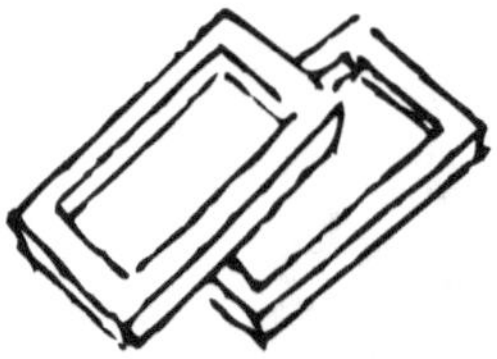

Staple a mesh screen to one.

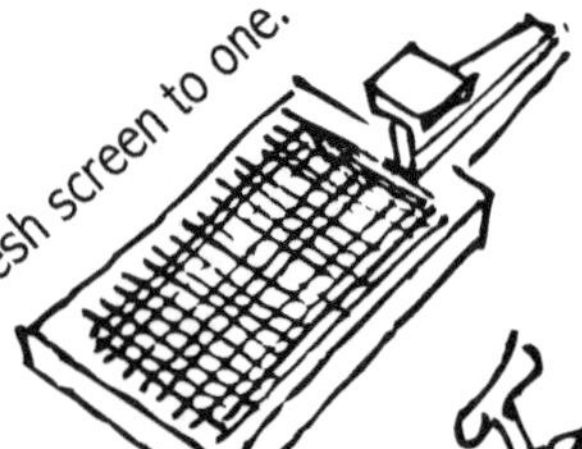

Tear newspapers into bits and put into warm water. You can add torn bits of cloth or other binding elements. That will add color flecks to your paper.

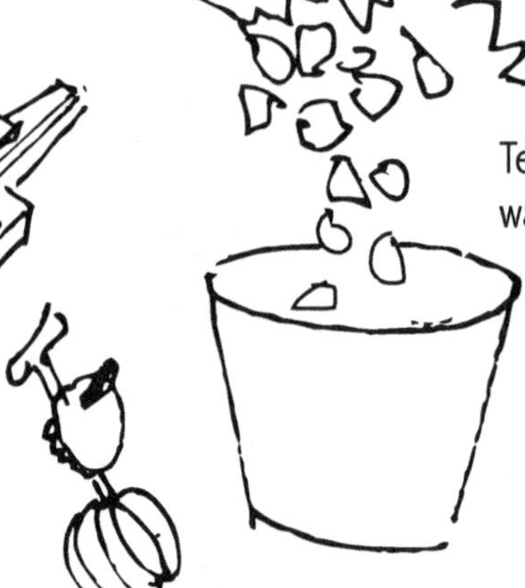

Place the frame with no screen on top of the one with the screen.

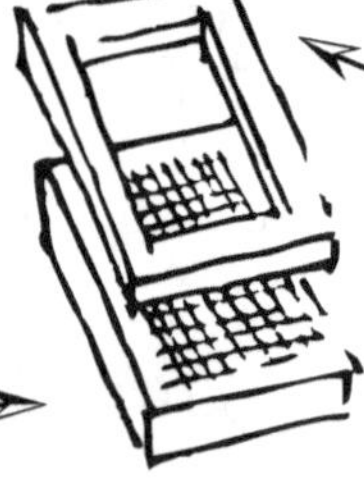

Use an egg beater to mix your paper pulp. Then dip into the pulp with the two screens. Lift slowly and then remove the top frame after the water has run out.

Make sense of your world by looking more closely at everything.

Turn the screened pulp onto a cloth to let it dry. You can iron it smooth when it is dry. You can trim the papers on a paper cutter or leave the edges rough (it's called decolletage

Find a shape somewhere. Use that shape as a pattern. See how many different ways you can make patterns from that shape.

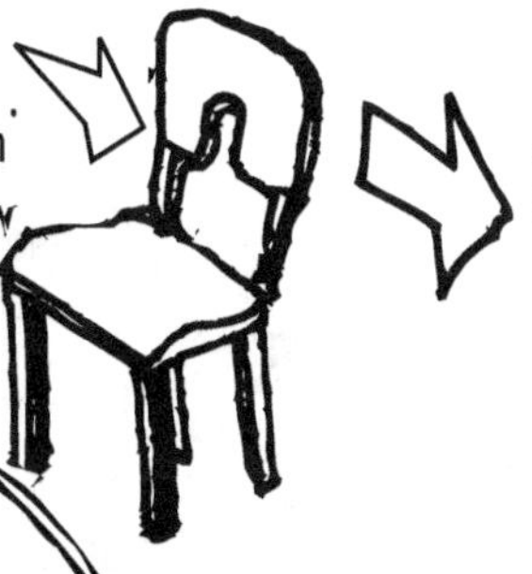

Change the shape to make your patterns better!

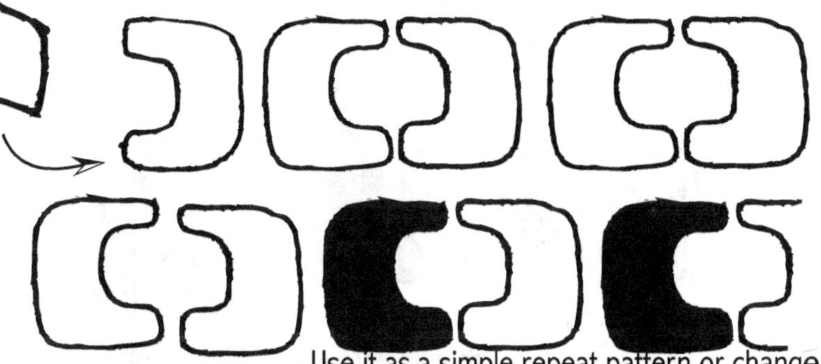

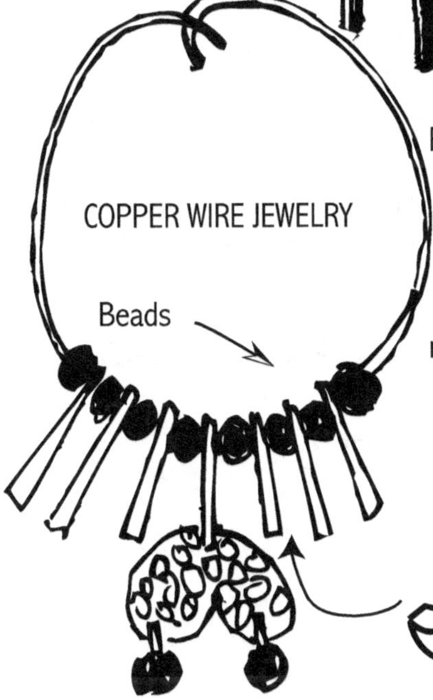

COPPER WIRE JEWELRY

Beads

Flattened short sections of copper wire with a hammer. Drill a whole or loop around the necklace wire.

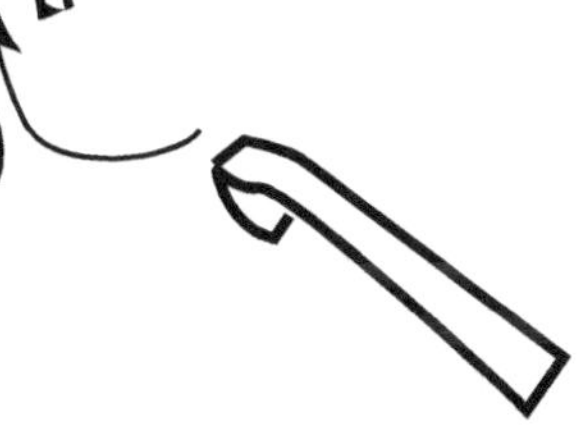

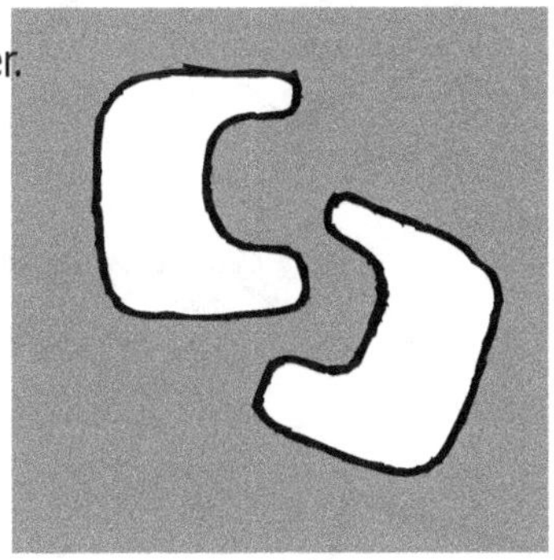

Use it as a simple repeat pattern or change its relationship or even use it in a different material

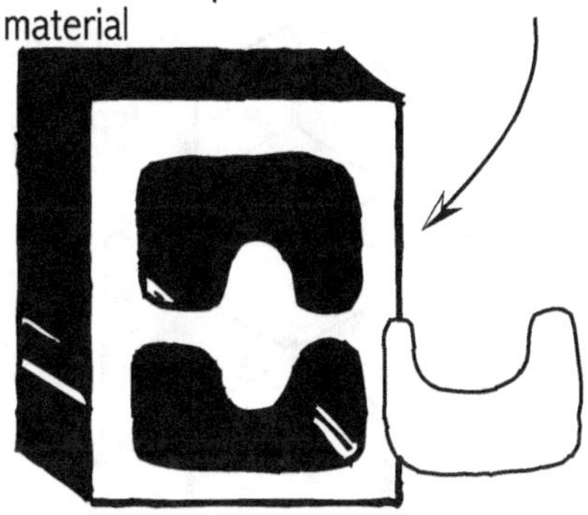

Take a short word and make it so the background is seen and read first. Make it so you can bounce between the positive and the negative.

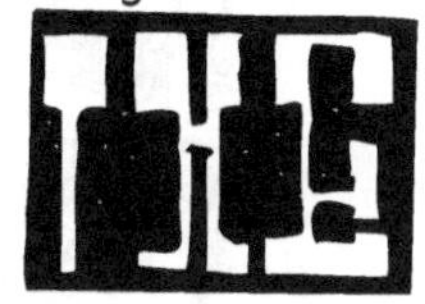

AESTHETIC JUDGMENT

Use words like shape, contrast, pattern when you talk about your work...make choices about your work, about the parts... Do you like your lines? Do you like the color? How is yours different from others? How would you change it next time?

ART 4

- ☐ Uses rhythmic variation to show line
- ☐ Uses shape and form, light and shadow
- ☐ Uses color values of dull/bright and warm/cool in work
- ☐ Uses overlapping and placement in space as perspective device
- ☐ Paints with water color, wet/dry brush techniques
- ☐ Makes simple figure drawings and still life
- ☐ Sculpts with additive and subtractive principles
- ☐ Makes collages of tissue paper, overlaps for transparencies
- ☐ Prints with roll-on, cardboard, or Styrofoam
- ☐ Weaves complex designs
- ☐ Recognizes changing room and community environments and relationships of past/present/future
- ☐ Differentiates originals and reproductions, and styles of art for similarities and differences

PLASTER SCRIMSHAW (Scrimshaw pieces were done by whalers on ivory tusks) Pour dollars size ovals of Plaster of Paris on the surface of a plastic covered table are on a sheet of plastic. Make the ovals a quarter to a half-inch thick. When they are dry, scratch on the flat surface with a compass point or a heavy pin. Rub black ink into the grooves.

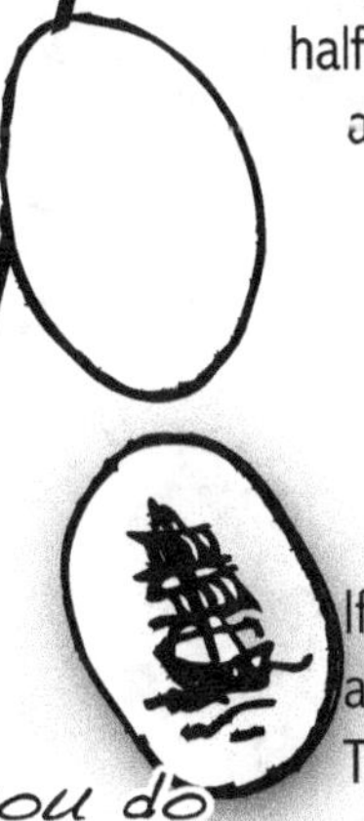

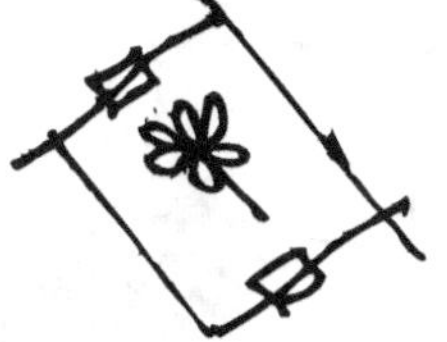

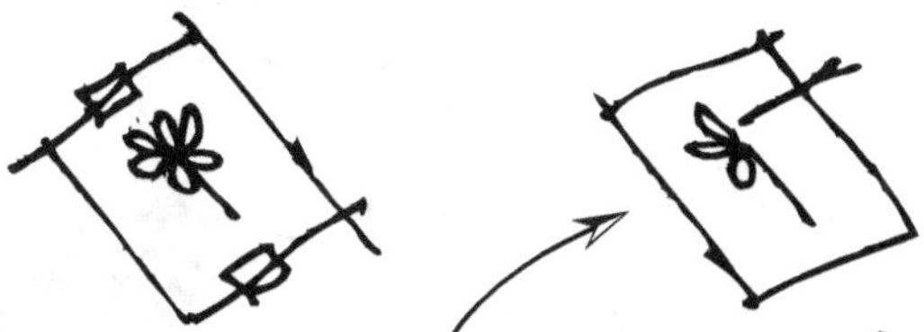

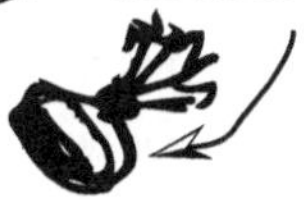

Ink dauber

If you like the results of that try etchings on acetate (such as the overhead projector film). Tape the acetate to your drawing. Scratch the lines with a needle or a sharp point. Make an ink dauber by putting cloth over some folded damp paper. Ink the lines with the Dauber. Lay dampened paper over the etching and Rub with a smooth block of wood.

Creative expression is what you do with what you see. It should show your uniqueness like a fingerprint.

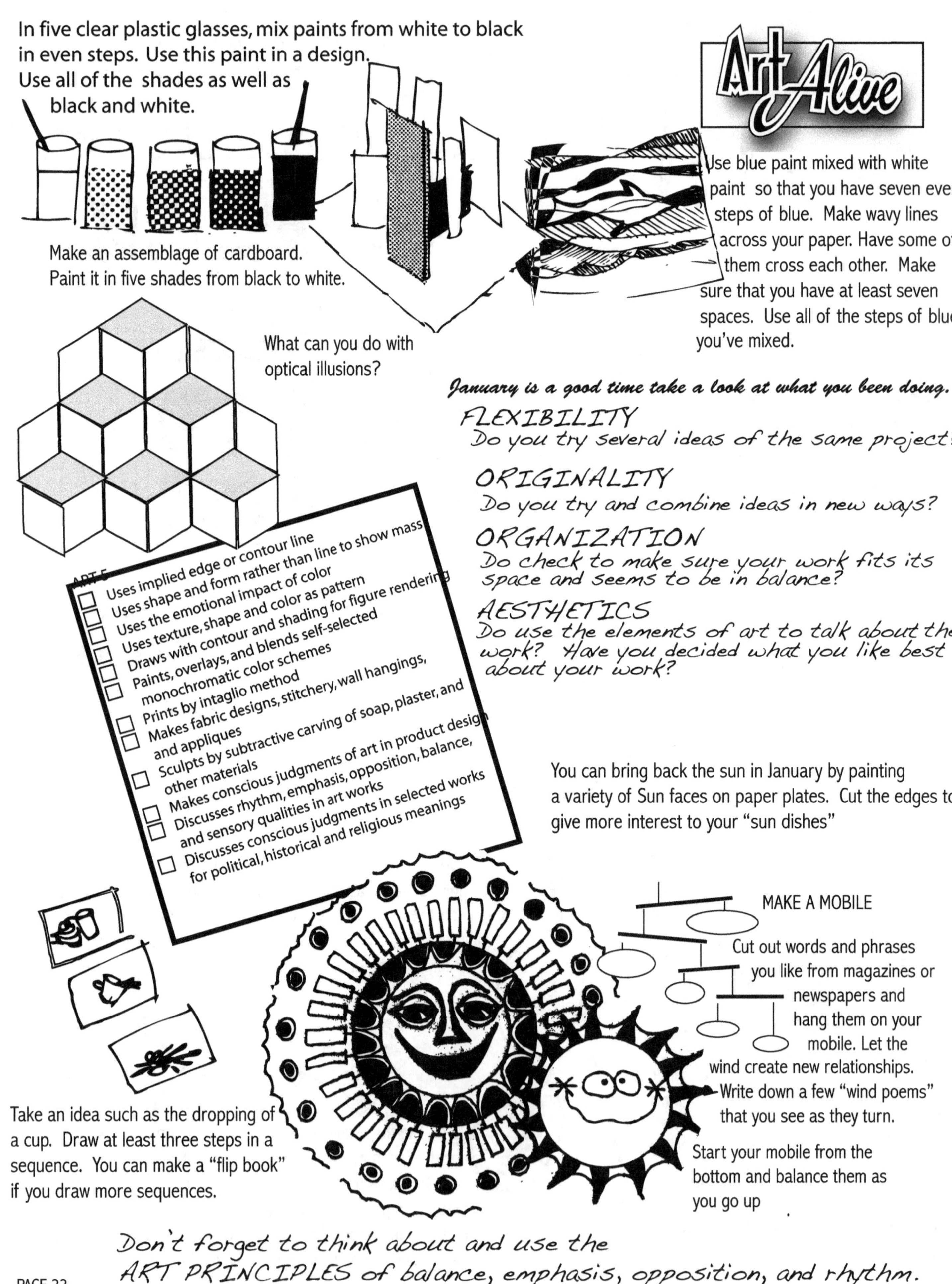

In five clear plastic glasses, mix paints from white to black in even steps. Use this paint in a design. Use all of the shades as well as black and white.

Art Alive

Make an assemblage of cardboard. Paint it in five shades from black to white.

Use blue paint mixed with white paint so that you have seven even steps of blue. Make wavy lines across your paper. Have some of them cross each other. Make sure that you have at least seven spaces. Use all of the steps of blue you've mixed.

What can you do with optical illusions?

January is a good time take a look at what you been doing.

FLEXIBILITY
Do you try several ideas of the same project?

ORIGINALITY
Do you try and combine ideas in new ways?

ORGANIZATION
Do check to make sure your work fits its space and seems to be in balance?

AESTHETICS
Do use the elements of art to talk about the work? Have you decided what you like best about your work?

ART 5

- ☐ Uses implied edge or contour line
- ☐ Uses shape and form rather than line to show mass
- ☐ Uses the emotional impact of color
- ☐ Uses texture, shape and color as pattern
- ☐ Draws with contour and shading for figure rendering
- ☐ Paints, overlays, and blends self-selected monochromatic color schemes
- ☐ Prints by intaglio method
- ☐ Makes fabric designs, stitchery, wall hangings, and appliques
- ☐ Sculpts by subtractive carving of soap, plaster, and other materials
- ☐ Makes conscious judgments of art in product design
- ☐ Discusses rhythm, emphasis, opposition, balance, and sensory qualities in art works
- ☐ Discusses conscious judgments in selected works for political, historical and religious meanings

You can bring back the sun in January by painting a variety of Sun faces on paper plates. Cut the edges to give more interest to your "sun dishes"

MAKE A MOBILE

Cut out words and phrases you like from magazines or newspapers and hang them on your mobile. Let the wind create new relationships. Write down a few "wind poems" that you see as they turn.

Start your mobile from the bottom and balance them as you go up

Take an idea such as the dropping of a cup. Draw at least three steps in a sequence. You can make a "flip book" if you draw more sequences.

Don't forget to think about and use the ART PRINCIPLES of balance, emphasis, opposition, and rhythm.

IF YOU WANT TO UNDERSTAND A CULTURE LOOK AT THE EYES IN THE PAINTINGS AND IN THE SCULPTURE. WHAT ARE THEY LOOKING AT? IS IT THE FUTURE? OR ARE THEY LOOKING AT THINGS AROUND THEM?

In hieroglyphics this is a cartouche. The oval surrounds a name.

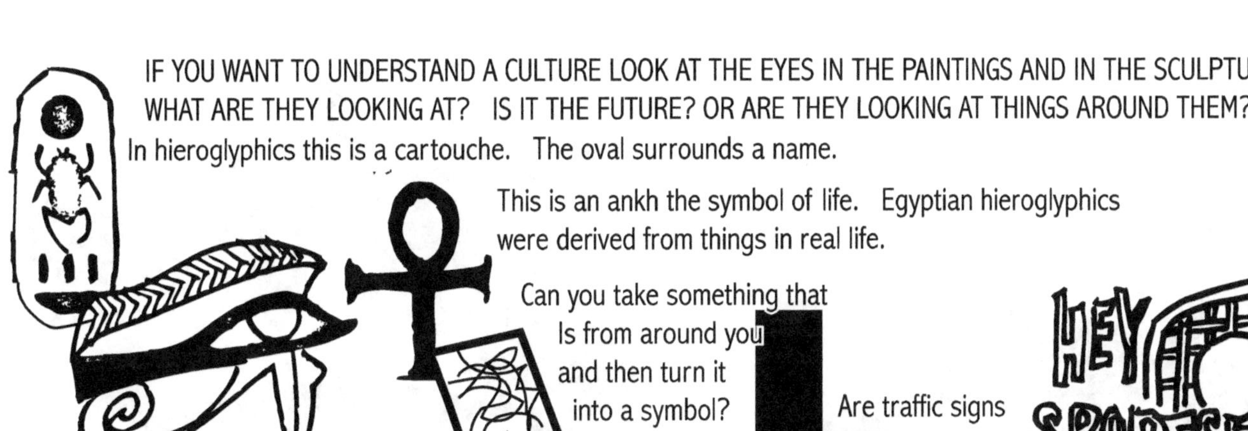

This is an ankh the symbol of life. Egyptian hieroglyphics were derived from things in real life.

Can you take something that Is from around you and then turn it into a symbol?

Are traffic signs like that?

This is the eye of Horus an important Egyptian deity

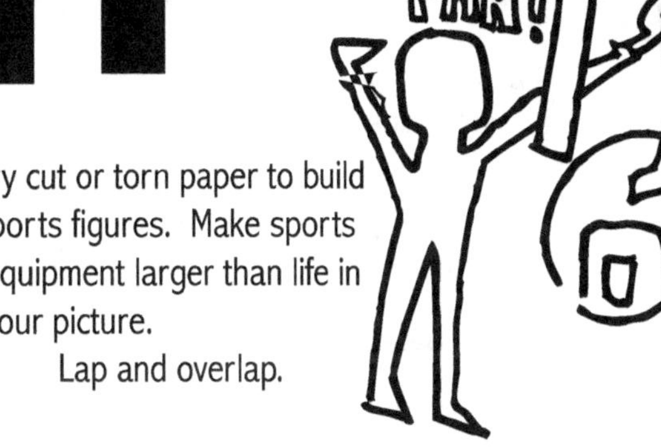

Cut or tear the colors of a season from magazines and build a montage of these colors.
Can you guess the season from your choice of colors?

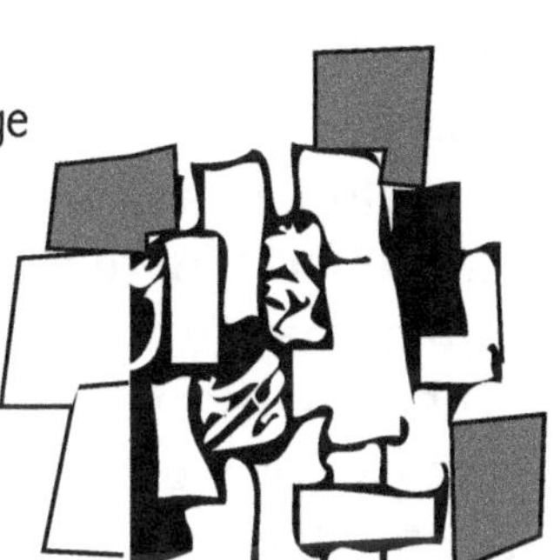

Try cut or torn paper to build sports figures. Make sports equipment larger than life in your picture.
Lap and overlap.

Make a doodle box to hold 3 x 5 cards. Doodle while you listen to stories or to music. Make a collection. Take one of your doodles and enlarge a section into a painting.

PERCEPTION:
We make sense of our world by looking. Many times our eyes and our mind fools us. Drawing a thing makes us look more closely.

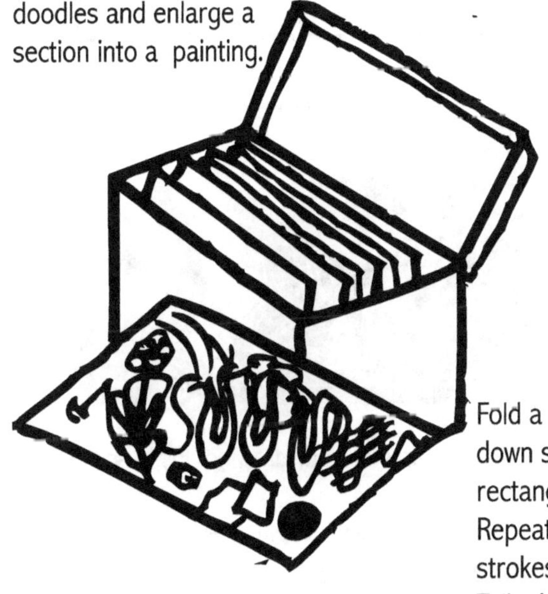

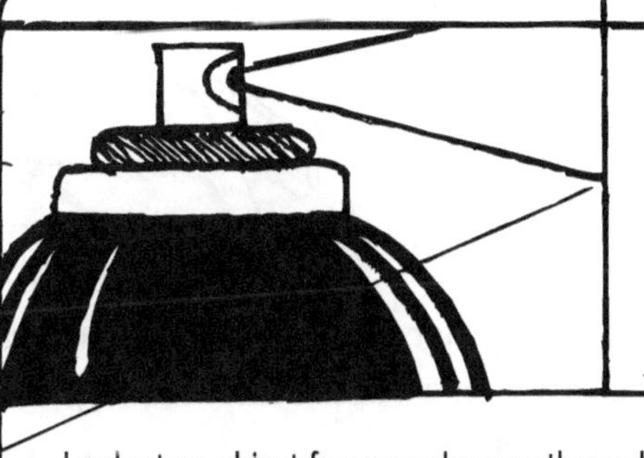

Fold a paper across and down so there are rectangles
Repeat the same brush strokes in each rectangle.
Talk about the patterns you make.

Look at an object from up close or through a frame held near to it. Draw what you see. Enlarge it ten to twenty times. Use a can of "Blow Up" spray and enlarge your world.

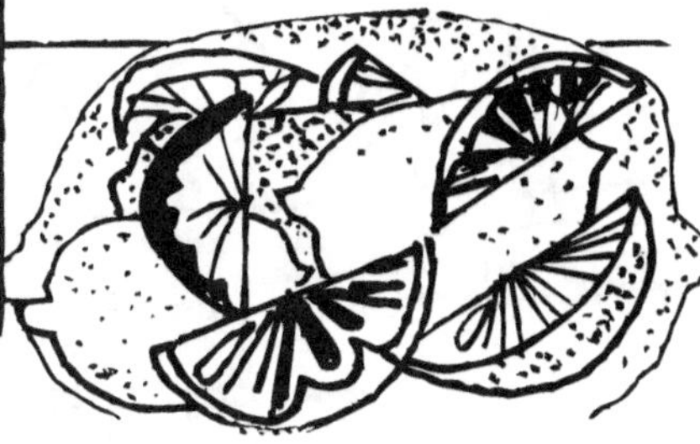

Cut apart a fruit like a lemon or an Apple and dra what you see as a design shape. Redraw in a var of ways. Overlap the shapes as you wish.

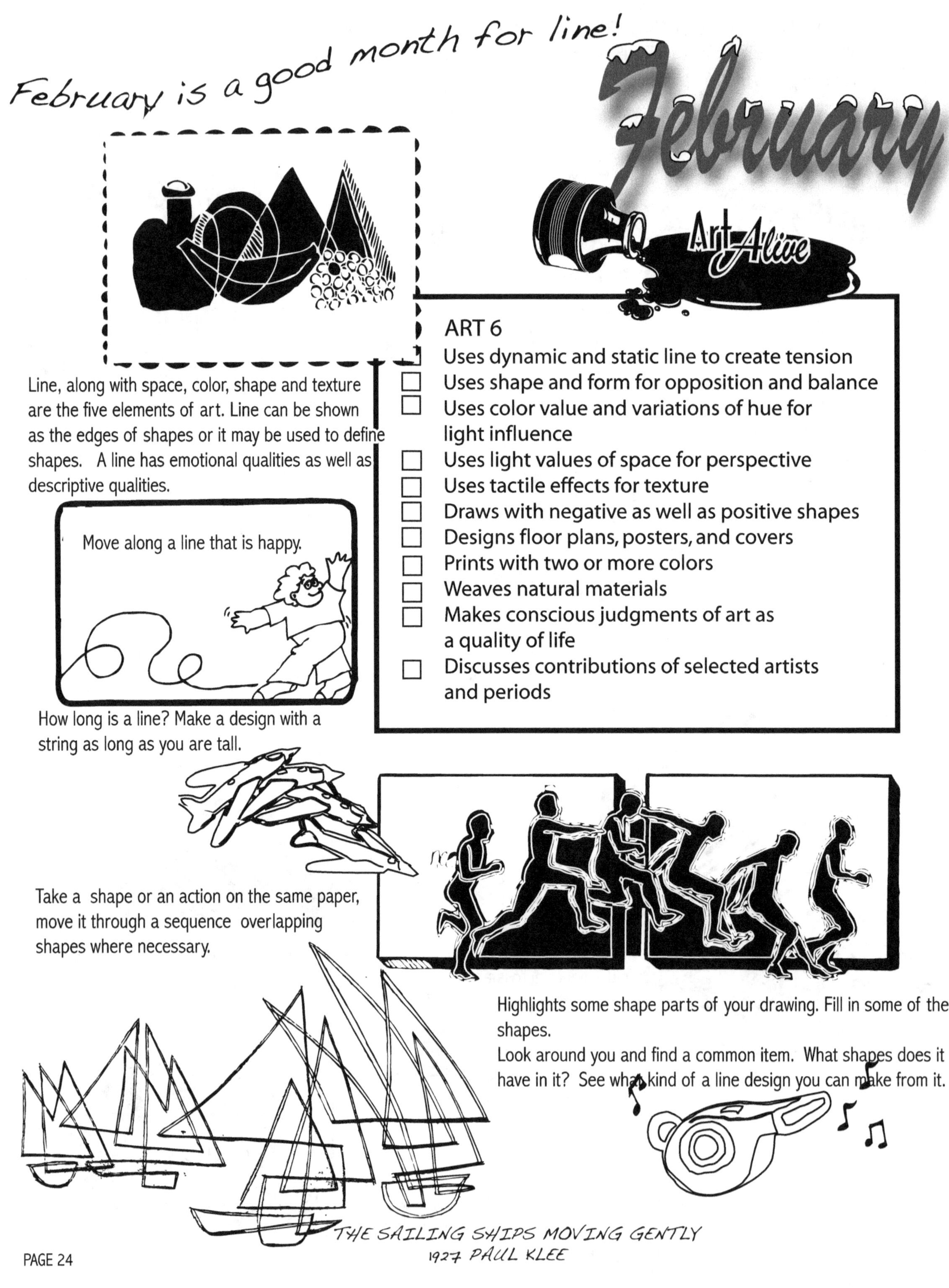

February is a good month for line!

February

Art Alive

Line, along with space, color, shape and texture are the five elements of art. Line can be shown as the edges of shapes or it may be used to define shapes. A line has emotional qualities as well as descriptive qualities.

Move along a line that is happy.

How long is a line? Make a design with a string as long as you are tall.

ART 6

- ☐ Uses dynamic and static line to create tension
- ☐ Uses shape and form for opposition and balance
- ☐ Uses color value and variations of hue for light influence
- ☐ Uses light values of space for perspective
- ☐ Uses tactile effects for texture
- ☐ Draws with negative as well as positive shapes
- ☐ Designs floor plans, posters, and covers
- ☐ Prints with two or more colors
- ☐ Weaves natural materials
- ☐ Makes conscious judgments of art as a quality of life
- ☐ Discusses contributions of selected artists and periods

Take a shape or an action on the same paper, move it through a sequence overlapping shapes where necessary.

Highlights some shape parts of your drawing. Fill in some of the shapes.

Look around you and find a common item. What shapes does it have in it? See what kind of a line design you can make from it.

THE SAILING SHIPS MOVING GENTLY
1927 PAUL KLEE

You can create hart mobiles by joining several heart shapes. It is more interesting if you use several colors.

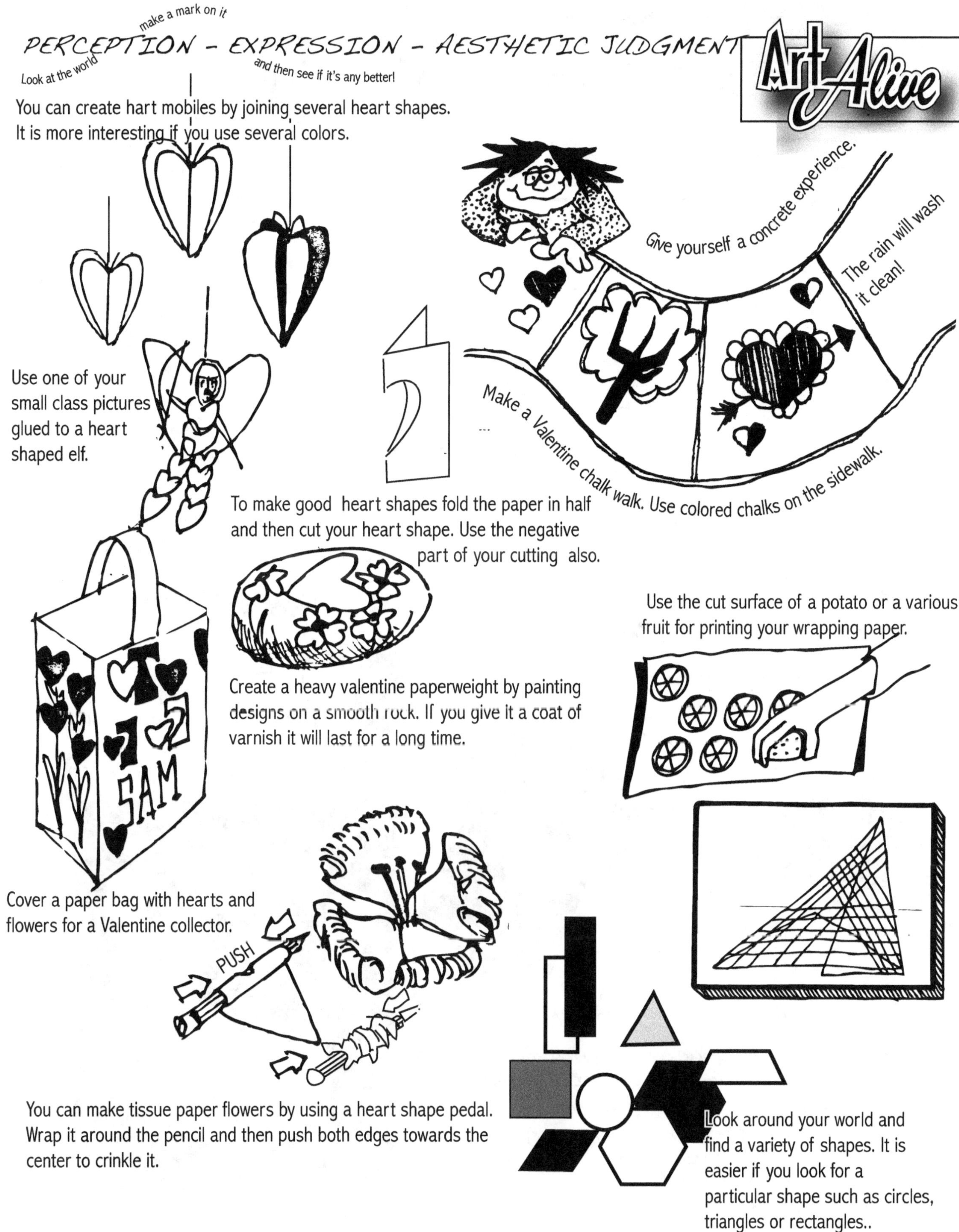

Use one of your small class pictures glued to a heart shaped elf.

To make good heart shapes fold the paper in half and then cut your heart shape. Use the negative part of your cutting also.

Use the cut surface of a potato or a various fruit for printing your wrapping paper.

Create a heavy valentine paperweight by painting designs on a smooth rock. If you give it a coat of varnish it will last for a long time.

Cover a paper bag with hearts and flowers for a Valentine collector.

You can make tissue paper flowers by using a heart shape pedal. Wrap it around the pencil and then push both edges towards the center to crinkle it.

Look around your world and find a variety of shapes. It is easier if you look for a particular shape such as circles, triangles or rectangles..

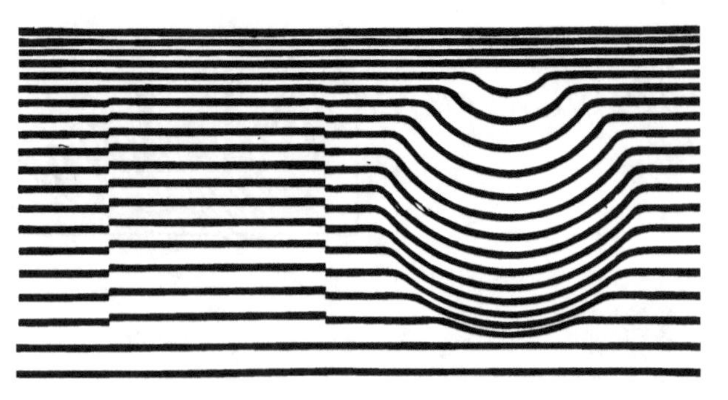

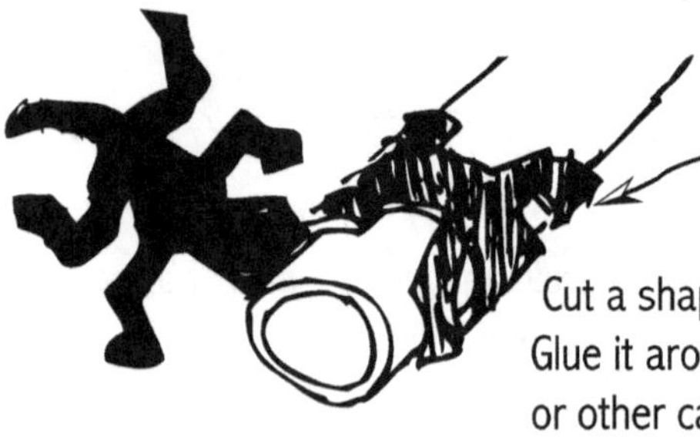

Cut a shape out of thin Styrofoam. Glue it around a mailing tube or or other cardboard tube. Ink your design with a brush or a sponge and roll out a series of patterns.

LOOK WHAT YOU CAN DO WITH LINES!
Shape and perspectives are an illusion created with the elements of art.

Use two papers of different colors. Placed together, fold and cut.

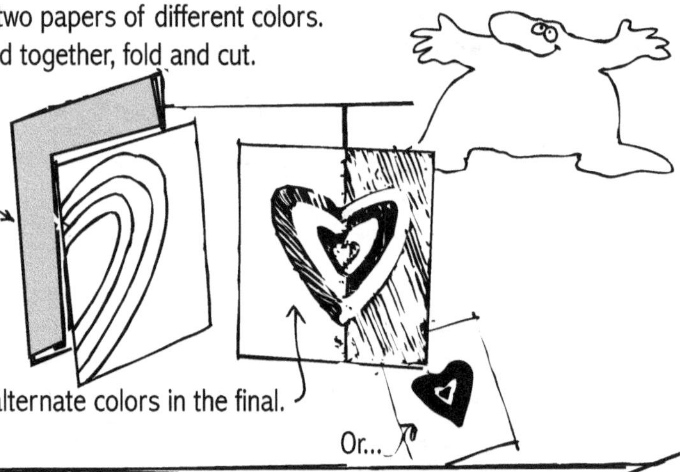

Use alternate colors in the final.

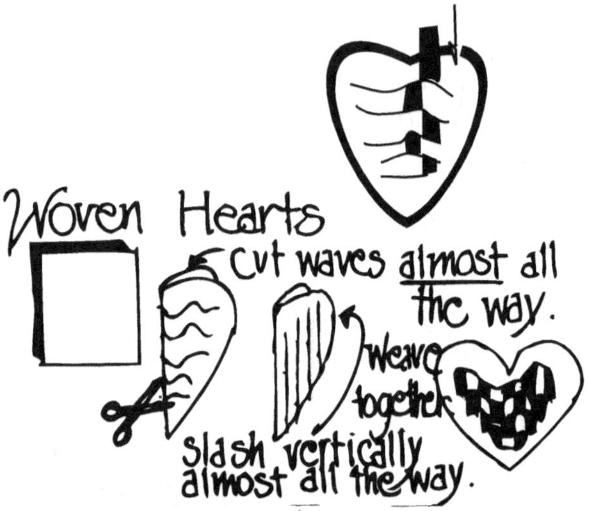

Or...

Woven Hearts

Cut waves almost all the way.

Slash vertically almost all the way.

Weave together.

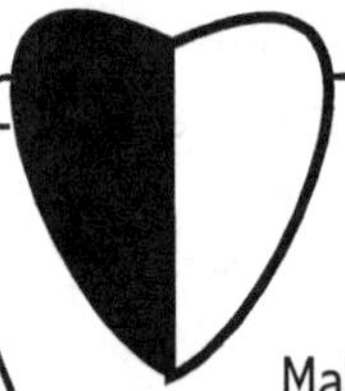

Pace two colored papers together, red and white or pink and white and cut out a variety of heart shapes.
Make one design the opposite of the other.

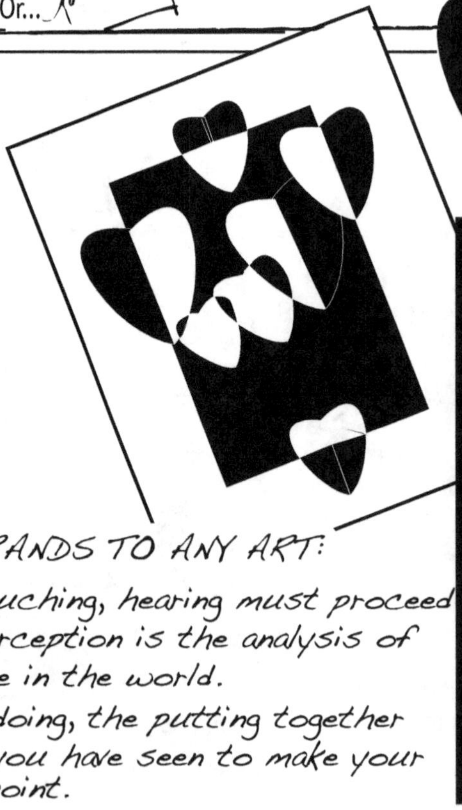

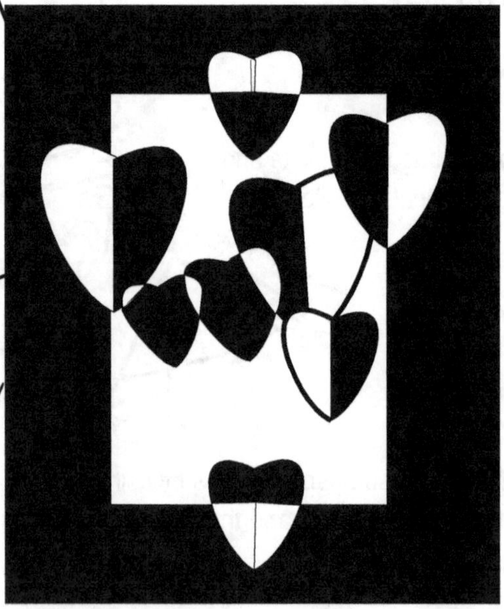

Art Alive

THERE ARE THREE STRANDS TO ANY ART:

PERCEPTION: seeing, touching, hearing must proceed the doing. Perception is the analysis of what you see in the world.

EXPRESSION: It's the doing, the putting together of what you have seen to make your new viewpoint.

AESTHETIC JUDGMENT: It's the necessary part of any activity, it's one's approval or disapproval of what's been done.

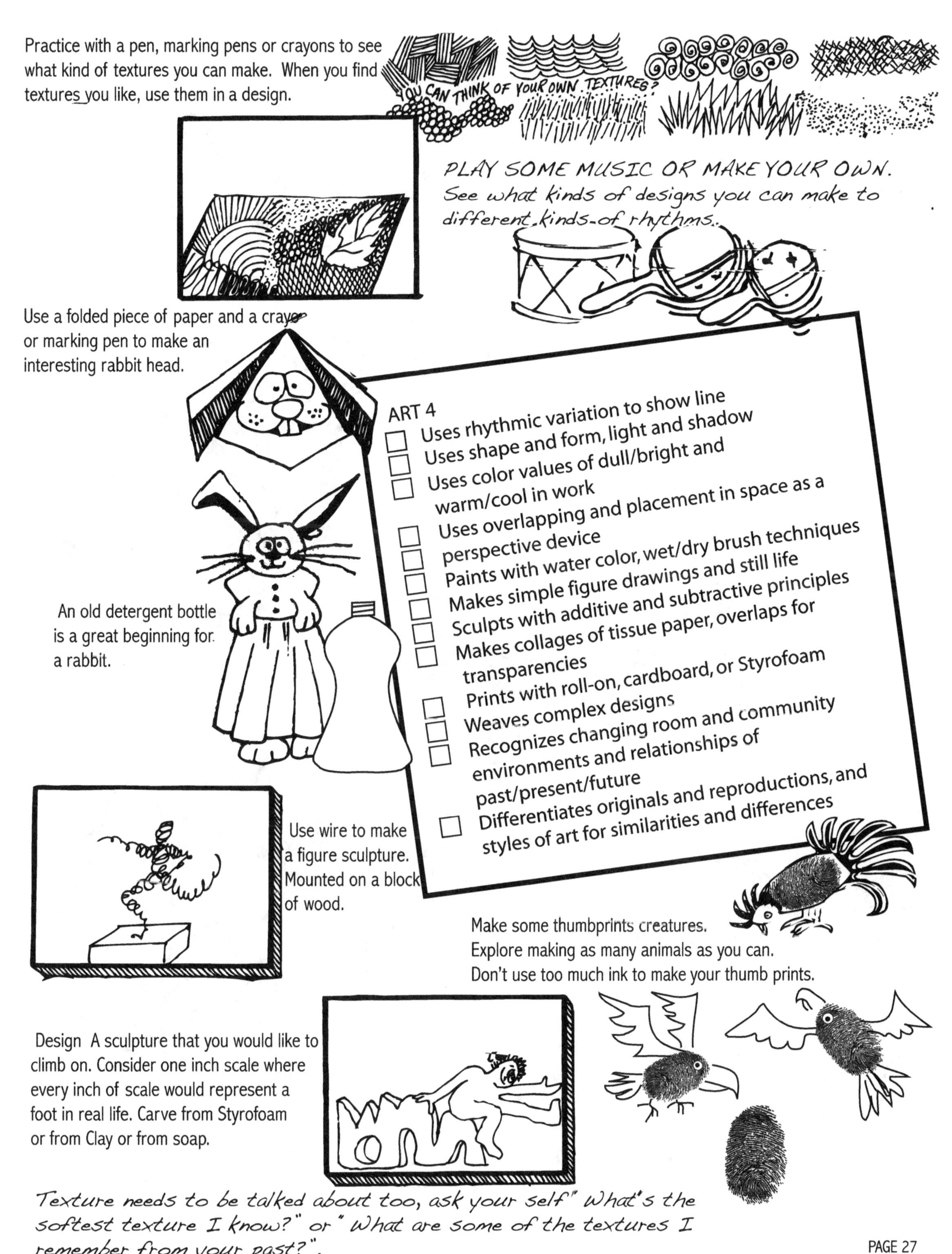

Practice with a pen, marking pens or crayons to see what kind of textures you can make. When you find textures you like, use them in a design.

PLAY SOME MUSIC OR MAKE YOUR OWN. See what kinds of designs you can make to different kinds of rhythms.

Use a folded piece of paper and a crayon or marking pen to make an interesting rabbit head.

An old detergent bottle is a great beginning for a rabbit.

ART 4

- ☐ Uses rhythmic variation to show line
- ☐ Uses shape and form, light and shadow
- ☐ Uses color values of dull/bright and warm/cool in work
- ☐ Uses overlapping and placement in space as a perspective device
- ☐ Paints with water color, wet/dry brush techniques
- ☐ Makes simple figure drawings and still life
- ☐ Sculpts with additive and subtractive principles
- ☐ Makes collages of tissue paper, overlaps for transparencies
- ☐ Prints with roll-on, cardboard, or Styrofoam
- ☐ Weaves complex designs
- ☐ Recognizes changing room and community environments and relationships of past/present/future
- ☐ Differentiates originals and reproductions, and styles of art for similarities and differences

Use wire to make a figure sculpture. Mounted on a block of wood.

Make some thumbprints creatures. Explore making as many animals as you can. Don't use too much ink to make your thumb prints.

Design A sculpture that you would like to climb on. Consider one inch scale where every inch of scale would represent a foot in real life. Carve from Styrofoam or from Clay or from soap.

Texture needs to be talked about too, ask your self" What's the softest texture I know?" or " What are some of the textures I remember from your past?".

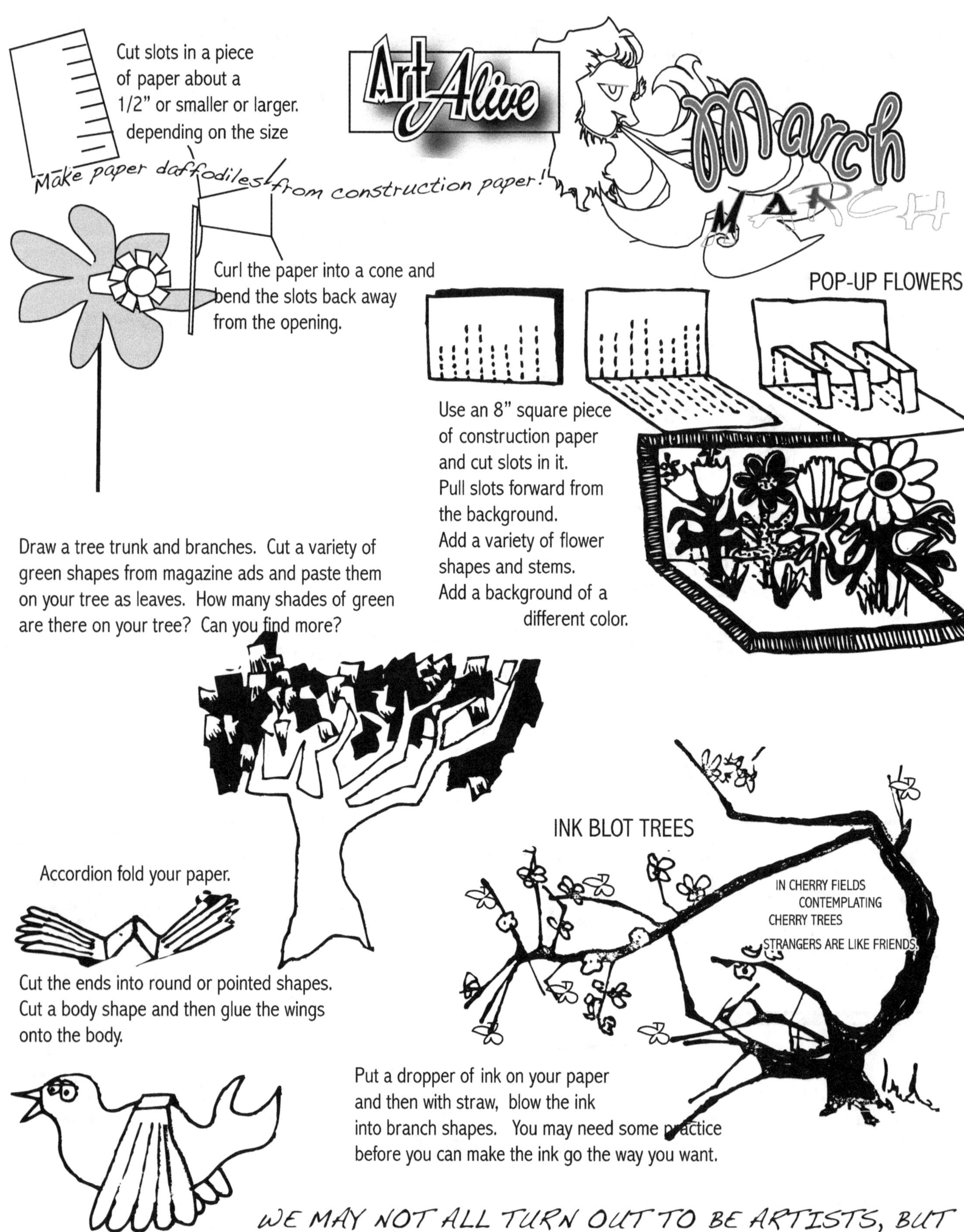

WE MAY NOT ALL TURN OUT TO BE ARTISTS, BUT WE SURELY ARE GOING TO BE CONSUMERS. REMEMBER, WE ARE WHAT WE CHOOSE... LET YOUR CHOICES BE BASED ON THE ELEMENTS OF ART.

BUNNY BASKETS

You can make bunny baskets or model trains from a simple fold of construction paper.

Leave a little extra on each end for a glue strip.

Cut and score with scissors on the center line of the ears

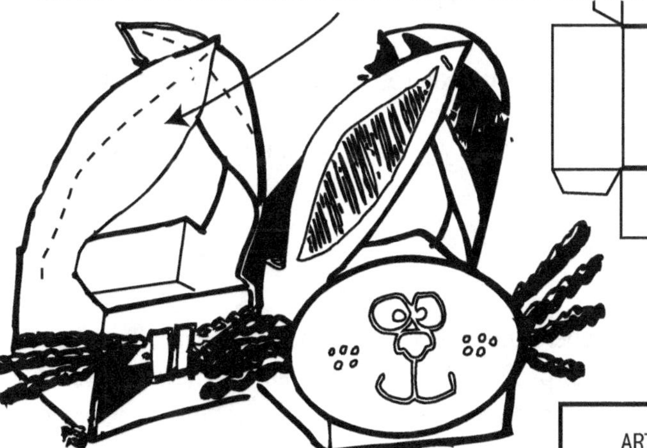

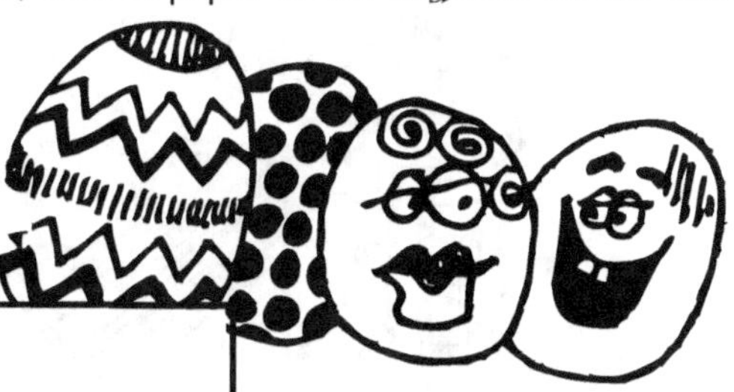

Use a straight edge to score the lines for the fold of the box. Add whatever details you wish, pipe stem whiskers, colored paper or marking pens for the ears.

ART 6th

- ☐ uses dynamic and static line to create tension
- ☐ uses shape and form for opposition and balance
- ☐ uses color value and variations of hue for light influence
- ☐ uses light values of space for perspective
- ☐ uses tactile effects for texture
- ☐ draws with negative as well as positive shapes
- ☐ designs floor plans, posters, and covers
- ☐ prints with two or more colors
- ☐ weaves natural materials
- ☐ makes conscious judgments of art as quality of life
- ☐ discusses contributions of selected artists and periods

Cut out several egg shapes and see how many different kinds of Easter eggs you can paint.

When you think you have been as original as you can be, then do one more.

Use a light source or a projector to project your shadow on a large paper. Have someone traced your outline in several athletic poses. Make sure the shapes overlap.

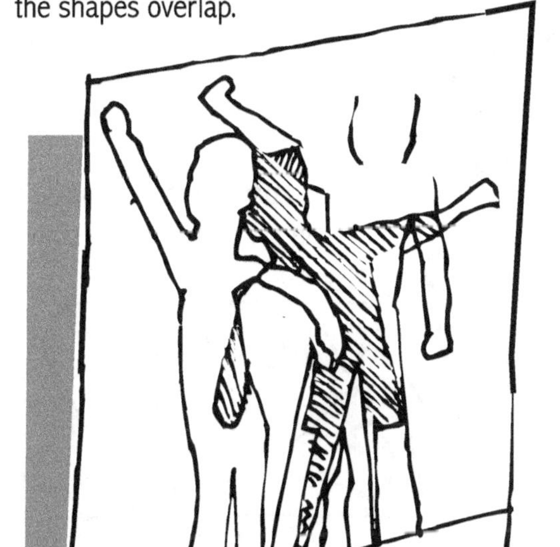

Break up the shapes into design areas. Fill them in with complementary colors.

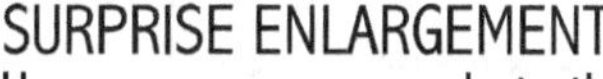

A1

A2

SURPRISE ENLARGEMENT

Have someone use a photo that you have not seen and mark the squares on the back numbering and lettering the rows and columns. Cut apart one by one draw what you see on the photo on a larger matrix of squares.

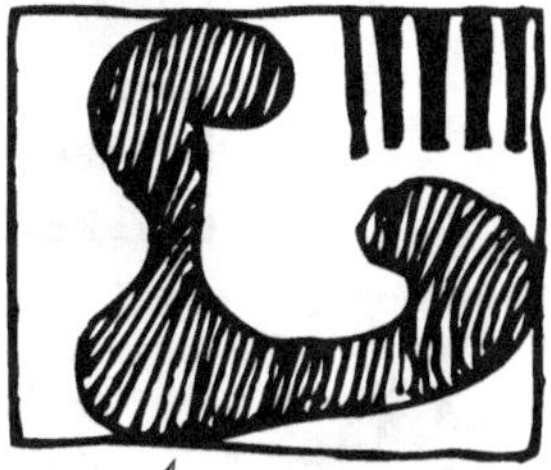

Use the interactive principles of rhythm, balance, opposition, and emphasis to make the elements of line, shape, color, space and texture work for you.

Keep the same position of the squares. Don't start with too many squares of a photo unless you're working a lot of friends.

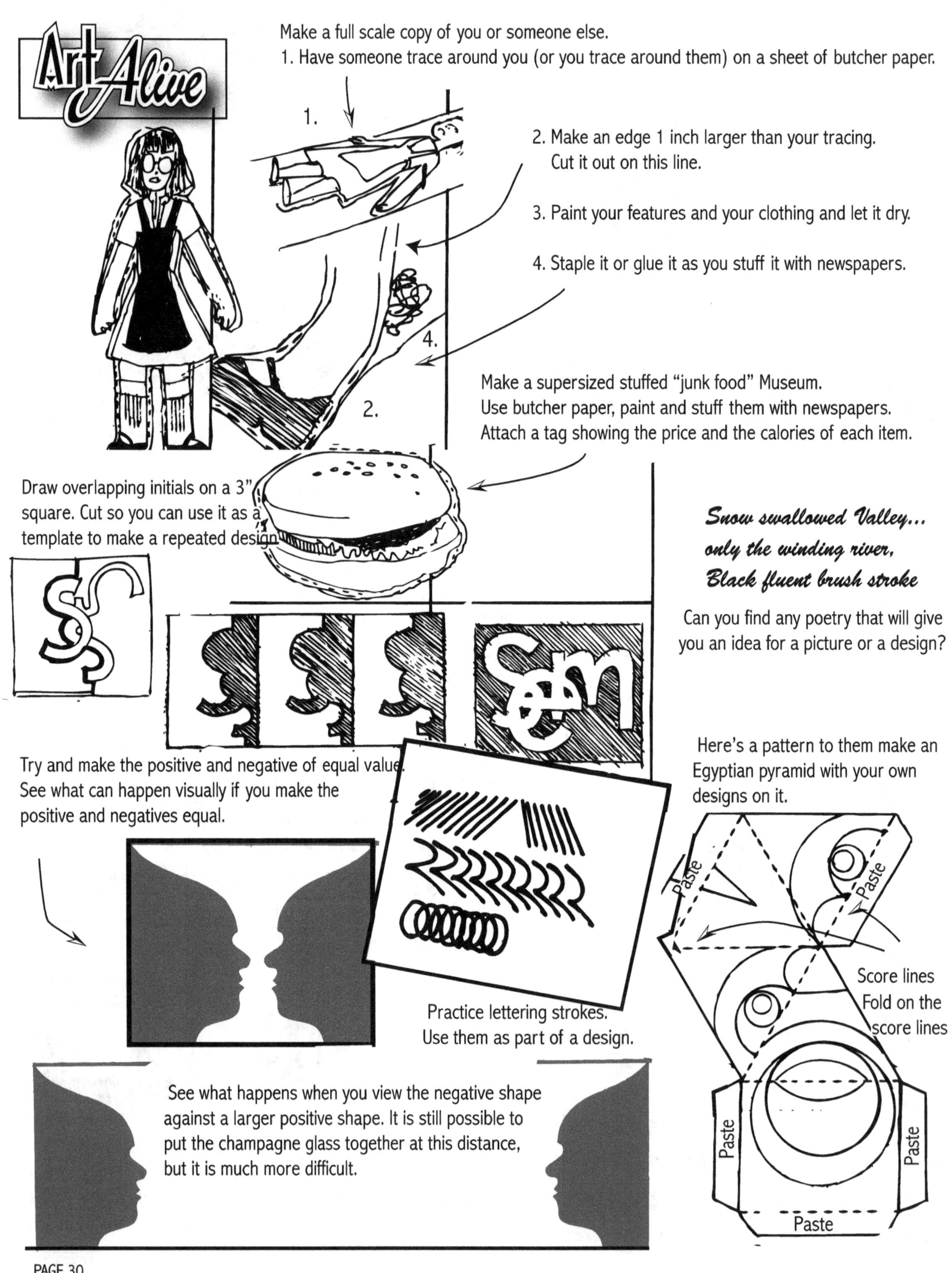
Art Alive
Make a full scale copy of you or someone else.
1. Have someone trace around you (or you trace around them) on a sheet of butcher paper.
1.
2. Make an edge 1 inch larger than your tracing. Cut it out on this line.
3. Paint your features and your clothing and let it dry.
4. Staple it or glue it as you stuff it with newspapers.
4.
2.
Make a supersized stuffed "junk food" Museum.
Use butcher paper, paint and stuff them with newspapers.
Attach a tag showing the price and the calories of each item.
Draw overlapping initials on a 3" square. Cut so you can use it as a template to make a repeated design.
Snow swallowed Valley...
only the winding river,
Black fluent brush stroke
Can you find any poetry that will give you an idea for a picture or a design?
Try and make the positive and negative of equal value.
See what can happen visually if you make the positive and negatives equal.
Here's a pattern to them make an Egyptian pyramid with your own designs on it.
Paste
Paste
Score lines
Fold on the
score lines
Paste
Paste
Paste
Practice lettering strokes.
Use them as part of a design.
See what happens when you view the negative shape against a larger positive shape. It is still possible to put the champagne glass together at this distance, but it is much more difficult.

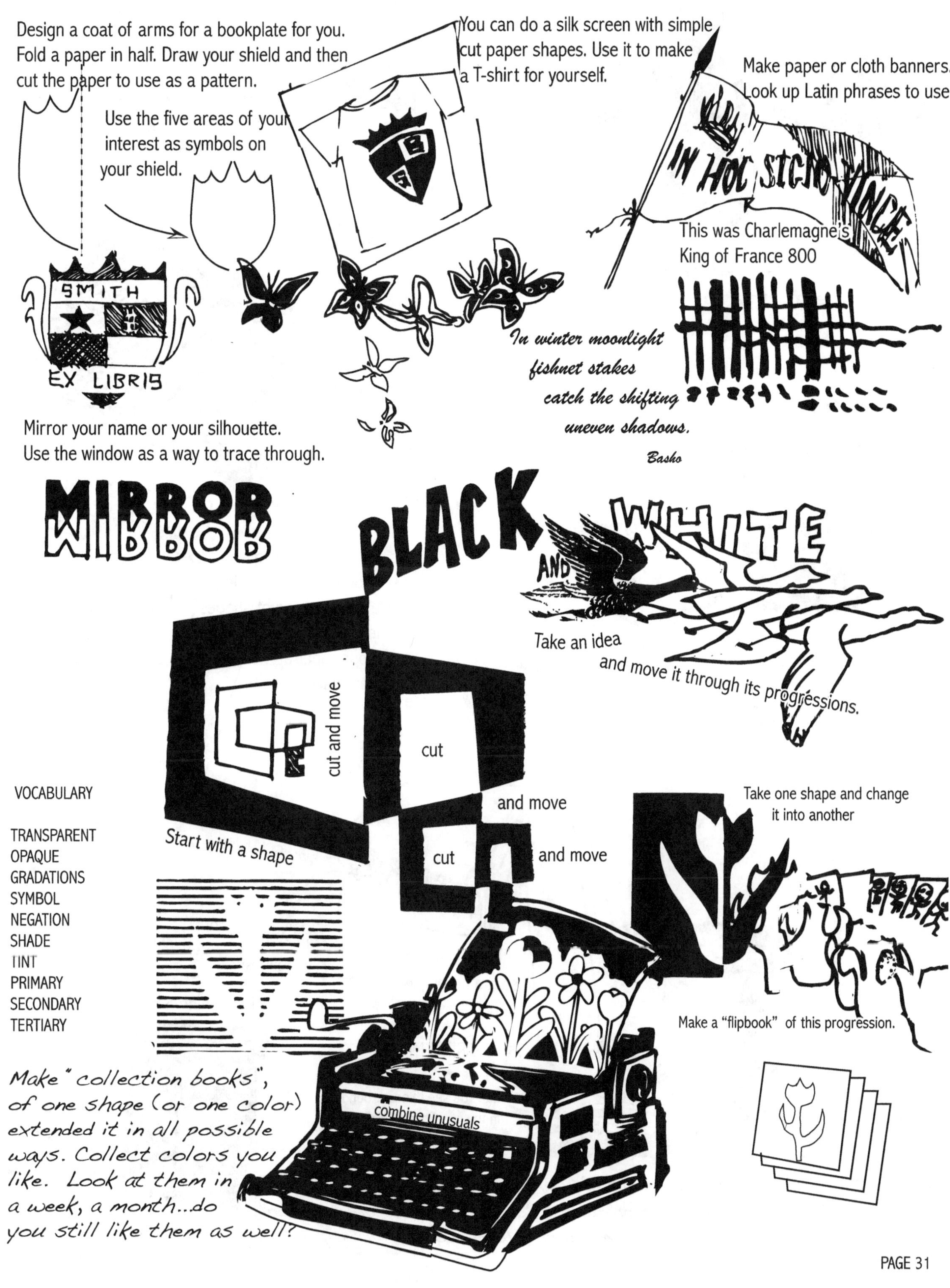
Design a coat of arms for a bookplate for you. Fold a paper in half. Draw your shield and then cut the paper to use as a pattern.
Use the five areas of your interest as symbols on your shield.
SMITH
EX LIBRIS
You can do a silk screen with simple cut paper shapes. Use it to make a T-shirt for yourself.
Make paper or cloth banners. Look up Latin phrases to use.
IN HOC SIGNO VINCE
This was Charlemagne's King of France 800
In winter moonlight
fishnet stakes
catch the shifting
uneven shadows.
Basho
Mirror your name or your silhouette. Use the window as a way to trace through.
MIRROR
BLACK AND WHITE
Take an idea and move it through its progressions.
cut and move
cut
and move
cut
and move
Start with a shape
Take one shape and change it into another
Make a "flipbook" of this progression.
VOCABULARY
TRANSPARENT
OPAQUE
GRADATIONS
SYMBOL
NEGATION
SHADE
TINT
PRIMARY
SECONDARY
TERTIARY
combine unusuals
Make "collection books", of one shape (or one color) extended it in all possible ways. Collect colors you like. Look at them in a week, a month...do you still like them as well?

APRIL Art Alive

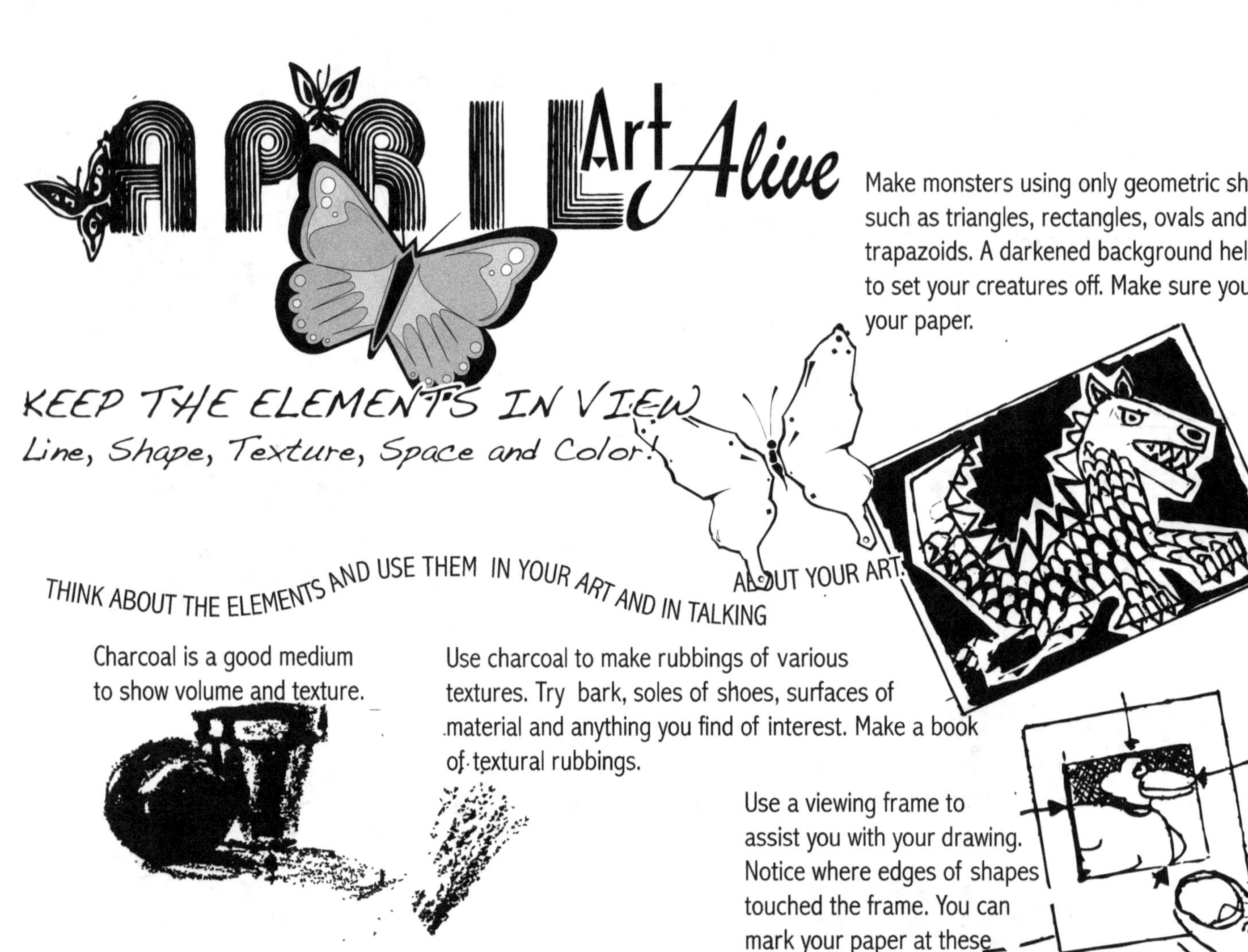

Make monsters using only geometric shapes, such as triangles, rectangles, ovals and trapazoids. A darkened background helps to set your creatures off. Make sure you fill your paper.

KEEP THE ELEMENTS IN VIEW

Line, Shape, Texture, Space and Color!

THINK ABOUT THE ELEMENTS AND USE THEM IN YOUR ART AND IN TALKING ABOUT YOUR ART.

Charcoal is a good medium to show volume and texture.

Use charcoal to make rubbings of various textures. Try bark, soles of shoes, surfaces of material and anything you find of interest. Make a book of textural rubbings.

Use a viewing frame to assist you with your drawing. Notice where edges of shapes touched the frame. You can mark your paper at these important parts.

The dinosaurs are not all dead. I saw one raise its iron head to watch me walking down the road beyond our house today. It's jaws were dripping a load of earth and grass that it had cropped.

It must have heard me where I stopped, snorted white steam my way and stretched its long neck out to see and grined quite amiably.

CHARLES MALAM

Can you see things around you in the way Charles Malam has seen the steam shovel?

Try turning a picture upside down. It will help you see.

PERCEPTION: What you see through your mind's eye.
EXPRESSION: How you show what you see and what you feel.
JUDGMENT: The choices you make of elements and principles in your works.

Pop-up books are easy and fun to make.

Try a sample first so you can see how it works. Fold the "pop-up" center so it is in the middle of the card. Paste tabs and then fold the card. Make sure it works as you want it to.

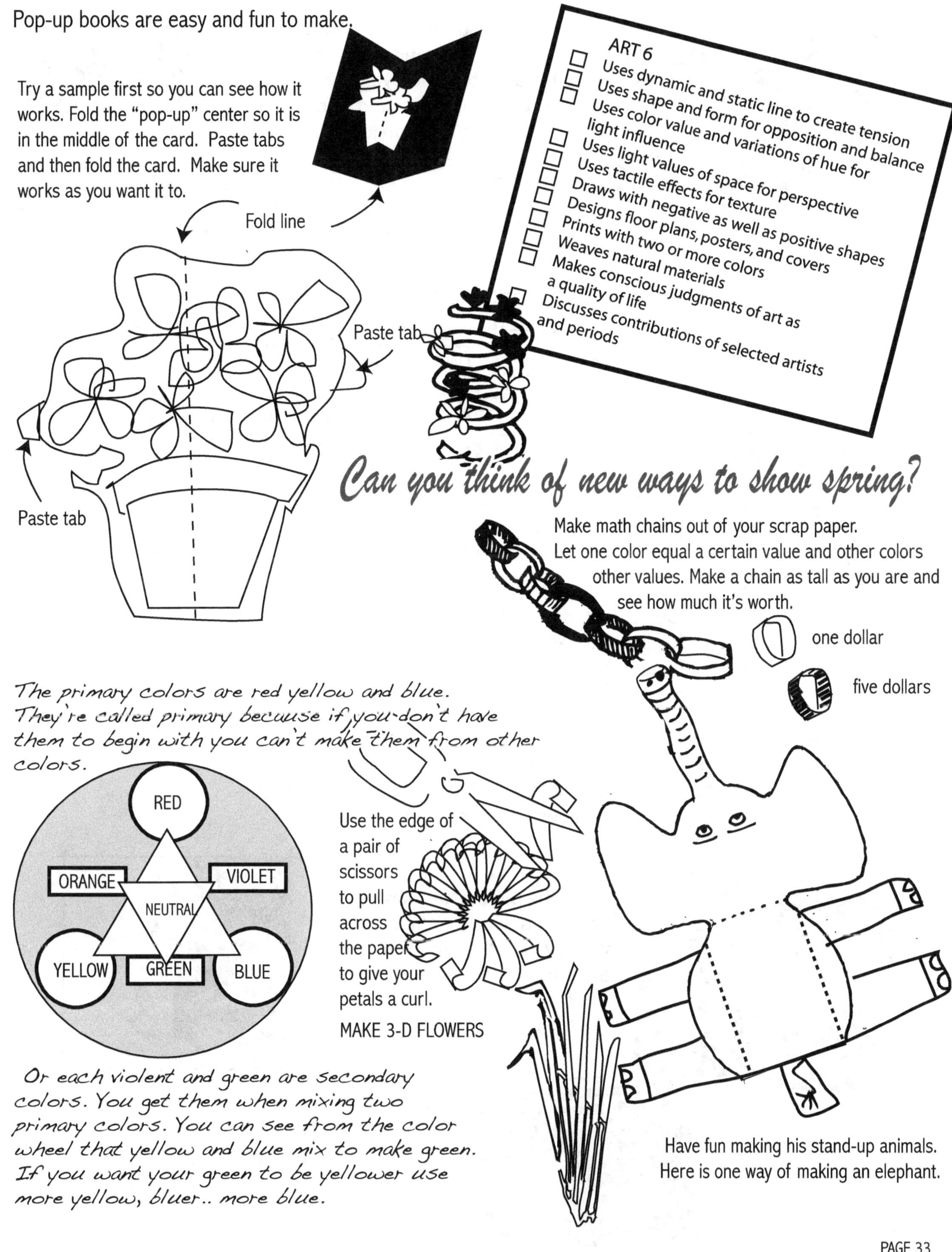

Make math chains out of your scrap paper. Let one color equal a certain value and other colors other values. Make a chain as tall as you are and see how much it's worth.

The primary colors are red yellow and blue. They're called primary because if you don't have them to begin with you can't make them from other colors.

Use the edge of a pair of scissors to pull across the paper to give your petals a curl.

MAKE 3-D FLOWERS

Or each violent and green are secondary colors. You get them when mixing two primary colors. You can see from the color wheel that yellow and blue mix to make green. If you want your green to be yellower use more yellow, bluer.. more blue.

Have fun making his stand-up animals. Here is one way of making an elephant.

Art Alive

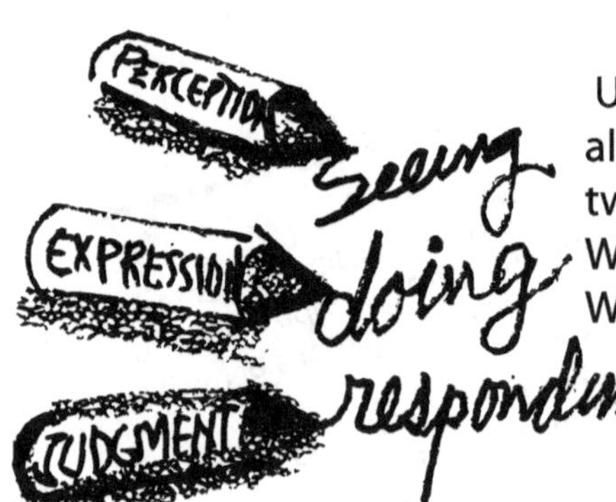

Use "dancing boxes" to generate new words along a theme. Start with one word, write down two words brought to mind by the first word. Write two words brought to mind from that word. Write a one-word combination joining of the two words.

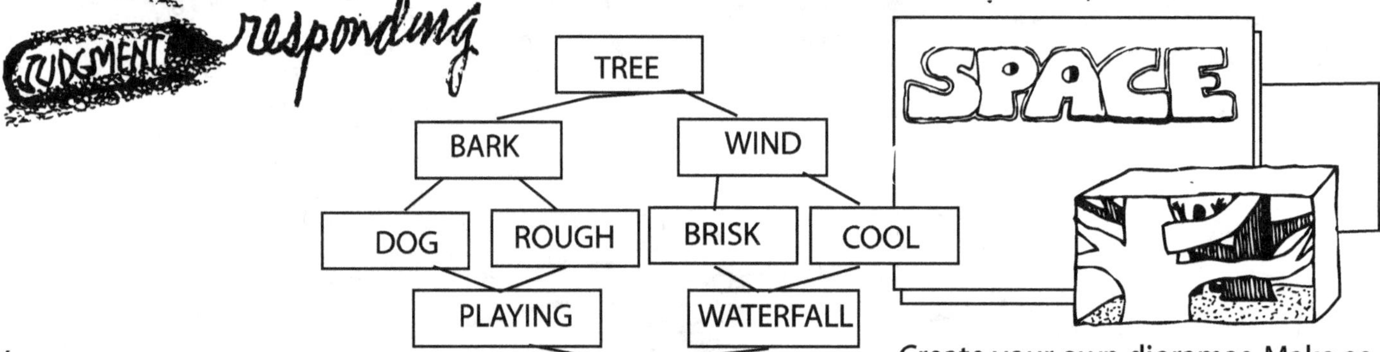

Is the last word like the first? You can use this process to write poetry or when you need ideas for a picture.

Create your own dioramas. Make as much use of the limited space of the box as you can.

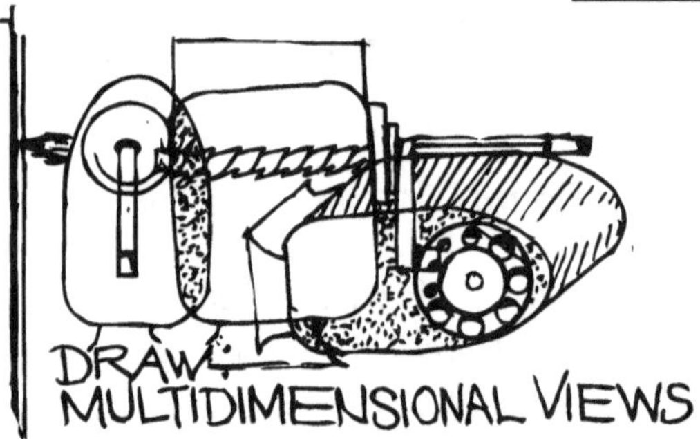

Take any common object and draw it first from the front and then in the same picture draw it from the side and the top. Include the function of the object in your work if you can.

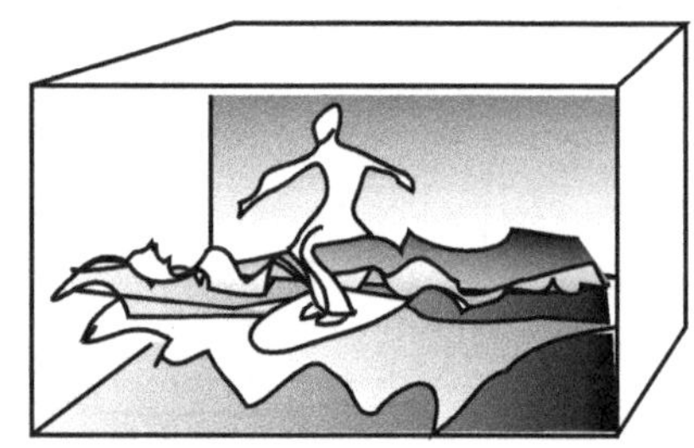

Use your own drawings or use cutouts from magazines. Most of the time it's best to do your own drawing.

You can use aesthetic judgment!
Find basic shapes in a picture. What colors were used? Do you like them?
Can you move into the picture? What does it feel like? Look at more paintings.
Do the paintings give you a clue as to what was important to the artist?

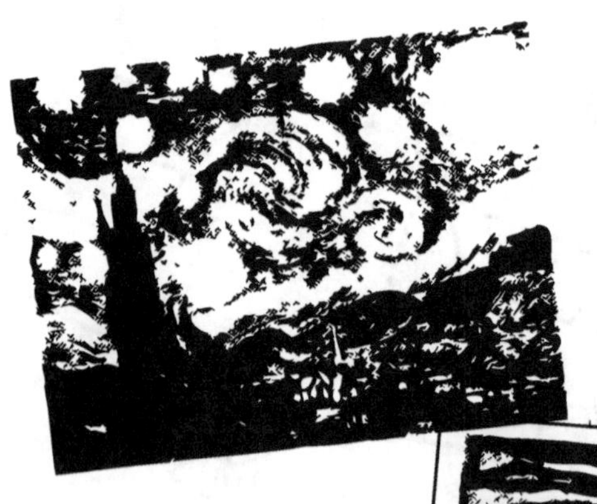

Does the picture tell any "truth" about your world? What can you say about the rhythm the artist used? Is the balance static or dynamic? Do you like the picture? Why or why not?

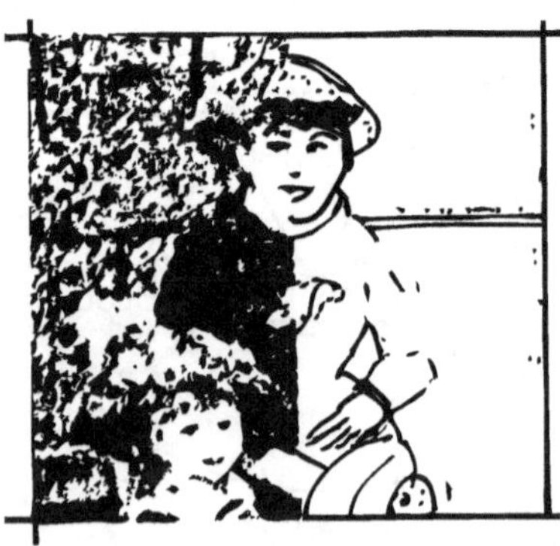

Take a picture you like from a magazine, cut it in half and paste it on another paper. Draw the other half of the painting.

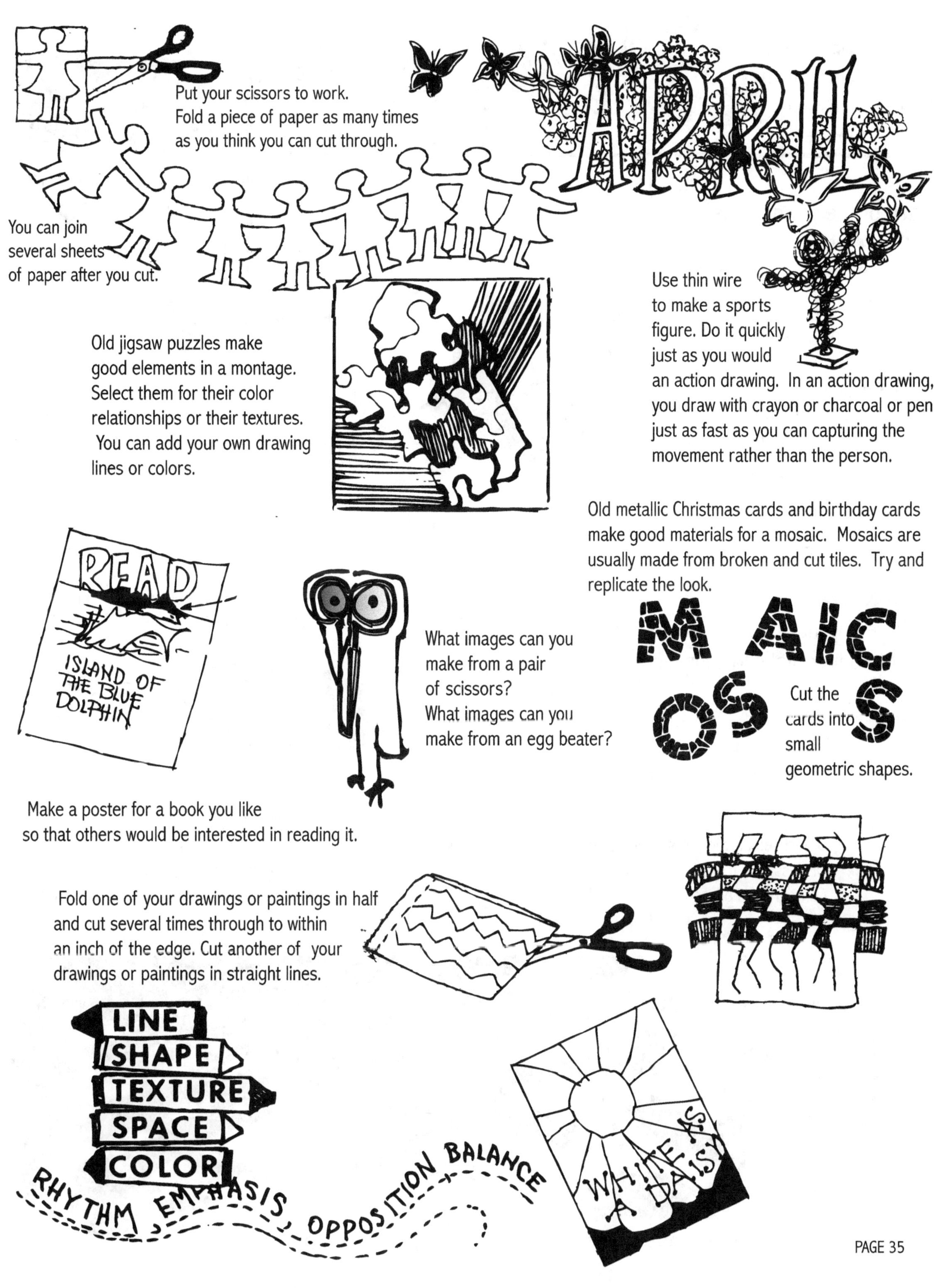

Put your scissors to work.
Fold a piece of paper as many times as you think you can cut through.

You can join several sheets of paper after you cut.

Old jigsaw puzzles make good elements in a montage. Select them for their color relationships or their textures. You can add your own drawing lines or colors.

Use thin wire to make a sports figure. Do it quickly just as you would an action drawing. In an action drawing, you draw with crayon or charcoal or pen just as fast as you can capturing the movement rather than the person.

Old metallic Christmas cards and birthday cards make good materials for a mosaic. Mosaics are usually made from broken and cut tiles. Try and replicate the look.

What images can you make from a pair of scissors?
What images can you make from an egg beater?

Cut the cards into small geometric shapes.

Make a poster for a book you like so that others would be interested in reading it.

Fold one of your drawings or paintings in half and cut several times through to within an inch of the edge. Cut another of your drawings or paintings in straight lines.

Three Strands
LOOKING (perception)
DOING (expression)
VALUING (aesthetics)

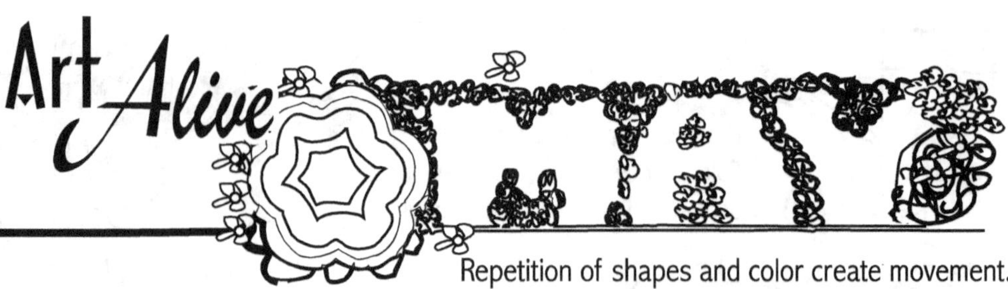

Each of the strands has:

Rhythm
What are the repeating elements? Does one shape echo and augment another?

Balance
The way in which the visual elements of the paper or sculpture seem to fit and do not appear lopsided or unequal.

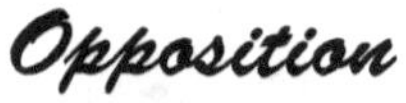

Opposition
Is there any interplay between elements? Light to dark? Static to dynamic?

Emphasis
Is the mood or intent of the work enhanced or made important by the selection of elements?

Repetition of shapes and color create movement.

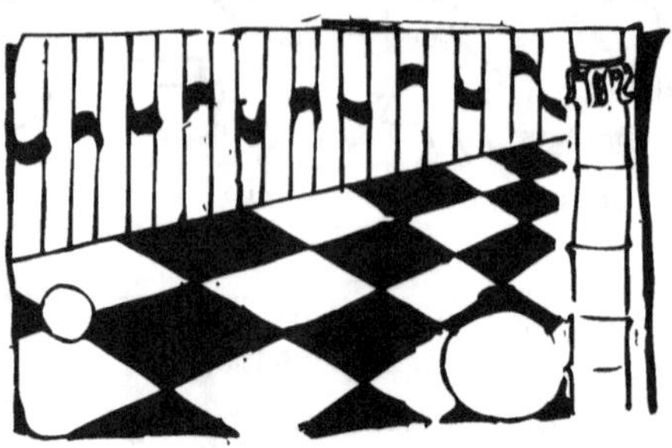

Listen to different musical instruments carefully. What shapes or colors or lines could be used to show their sounds? How would drums differ from violins?

Make a design or picture to a particular piece of music. Play the piece over several times before starting to work. Encourage Students to make idea sketches as they listen. Pay attention to the rhythm as well as to the harmony of the instruments. Can you use different design elements to show this?

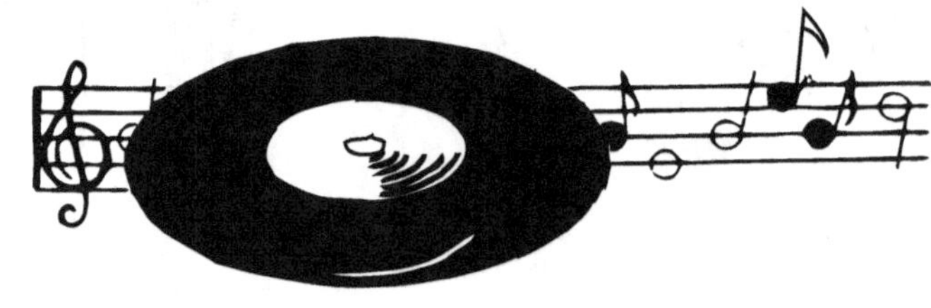

TREES/ LANDSCAPES

Objective: learning to see and to draw more accurately through looking at and drawing trees.
Discuss how trees like Spruce, Pine, and Sycamore differ from each other. Show photos if possible.
Compare the branches of trees, shrubs and flowers. After discussion have the students draw several tree pictures.

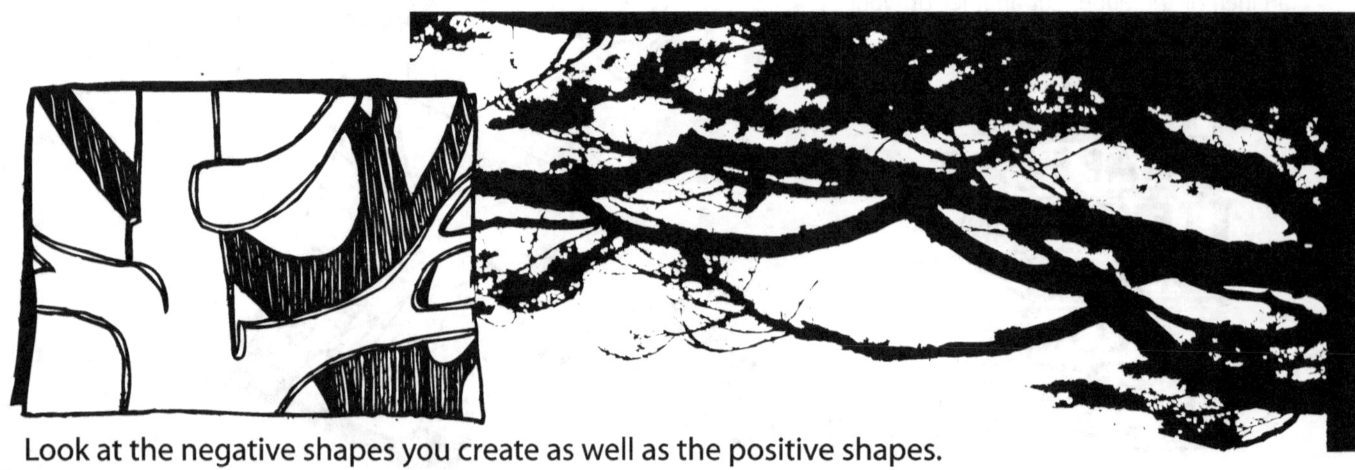

Look at the negative shapes you create as well as the positive shapes.

Van Gogh "owns" Irises for me because he has captured in his paintings their essence and spirit. Each Iris I see, is enriched for me through the eyes and paint brush of Vincent....

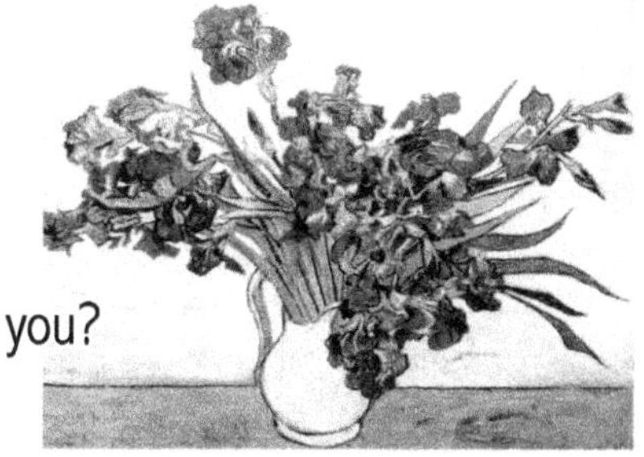

Does anyone own Spring for you?

ART 6

- ☐ uses dynamic and static line to create tension
- ☐ uses shape and form for opposition and balance
- ☐ uses color value and variations of hue for light influence
- ☐ uses light values of space for perspective
- ☐ uses tactile effects for texture
- ☐ draws with negative as well as positive shapes
- ☐ designs floor plans, posters, and covers
- ☐ prints with two or more colors
- ☐ weaves natural materials
- ☐ makes conscious judgments of art as quality of life
- ☐ discusses contributions of selected artists and periods

You can use the objectives of the grade level to create projects. For example, "Make a poster for a verb". or, "Weave some straw through cut paper."

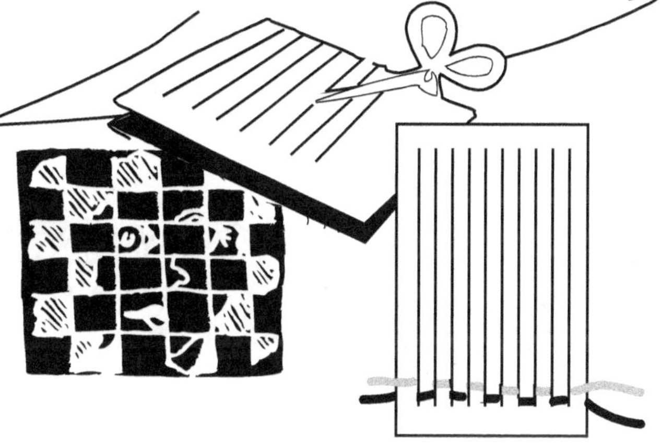

Drop a group of small stones or beans on a paper and mark where they fall. Use the mark to show you something to draw.

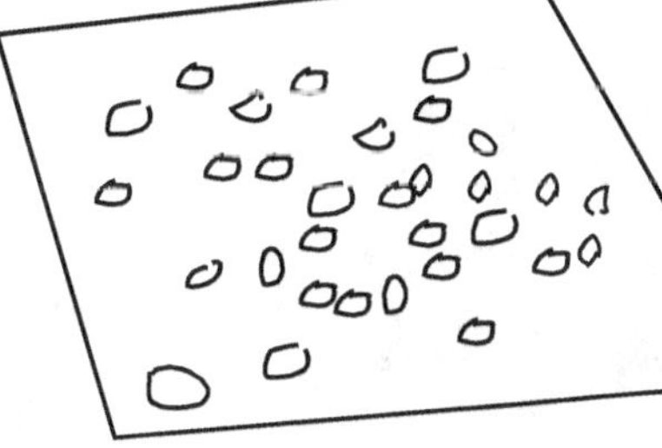

Cut a magazine picture into squares and reassemble into another picture or design.

Spring is like a perhaps hand (which comes carefully out of nowhere) arranging ...

Exert from e.e.cummings

USE THE BASICS LINE SHAPE TEXTURE SPACE COLOR

MIX AND STIR WITH

MIX AND STIR WITH

RHYTHM OPPOSITION BALANCE EMPHASIS

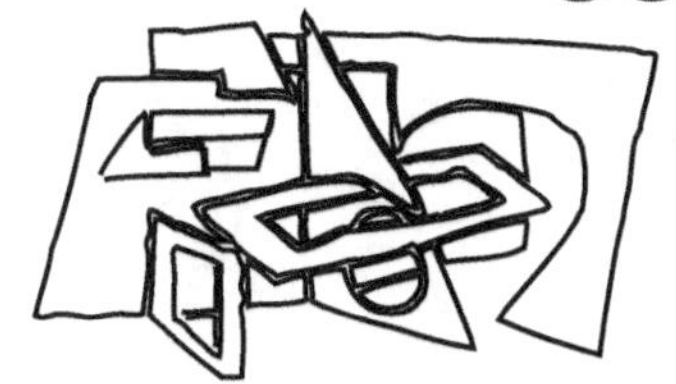

Some things changed with the season. Have you seen noticed some changes? Use some of the spring colors on odd scraps of cardboard and make a seasonal sculpture. Make up some new symbols for the season and use them in your sculpture.

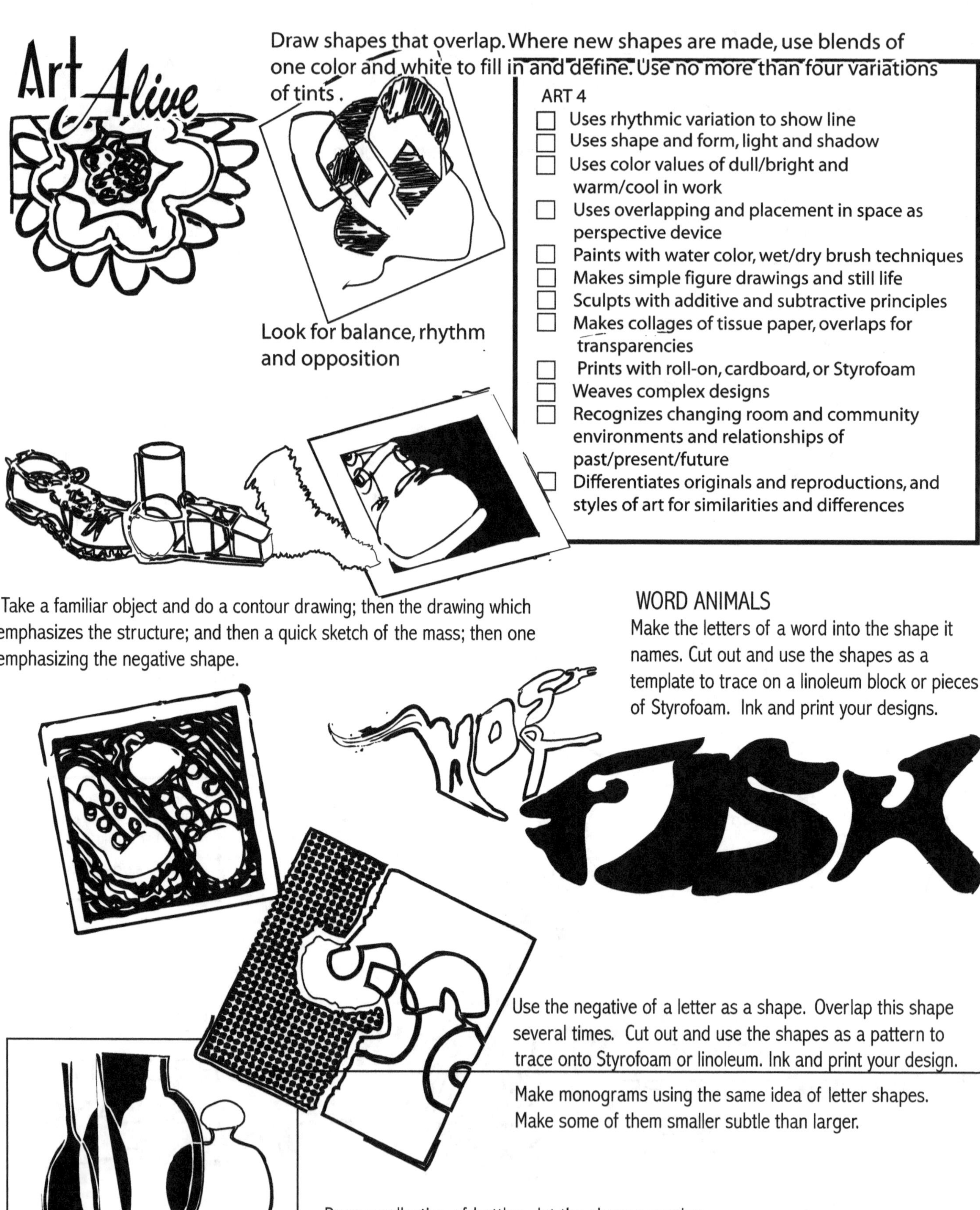

Draw shapes that overlap. Where new shapes are made, use blends of one color and white to fill in and define. Use no more than four variations of tints.

Look for balance, rhythm and opposition

ART 4

- [ ] Uses rhythmic variation to show line
- [ ] Uses shape and form, light and shadow
- [ ] Uses color values of dull/bright and warm/cool in work
- [ ] Uses overlapping and placement in space as perspective device
- [ ] Paints with water color, wet/dry brush techniques
- [ ] Makes simple figure drawings and still life
- [ ] Sculpts with additive and subtractive principles
- [ ] Makes collages of tissue paper, overlaps for transparencies
- [ ] Prints with roll-on, cardboard, or Styrofoam
- [ ] Weaves complex designs
- [ ] Recognizes changing room and community environments and relationships of past/present/future
- [ ] Differentiates originals and reproductions, and styles of art for similarities and differences

Take a familiar object and do a contour drawing; then the drawing which emphasizes the structure; and then a quick sketch of the mass; then one emphasizing the negative shape.

WORD ANIMALS

Make the letters of a word into the shape it names. Cut out and use the shapes as a template to trace on a linoleum block or pieces of Styrofoam. Ink and print your designs.

Use the negative of a letter as a shape. Overlap this shape several times. Cut out and use the shapes as a pattern to trace onto Styrofoam or linoleum. Ink and print your design.

Make monograms using the same idea of letter shapes. Make some of them smaller subtle than larger.

Draw a collection of bottles...let the shapes overlap. Use positive and negatives to accentuate your design.

You can enlarge any drawing.
Take the drawing that you wish to enlarge and make a grid suitable to the size of your final drawing. Use tracing paper or equal so you won't ruin the original drawing. Number the squares. Copy the shape that you see in each square of the small drawing into the large square of the same number.. You can modify the shapes as they are joined.

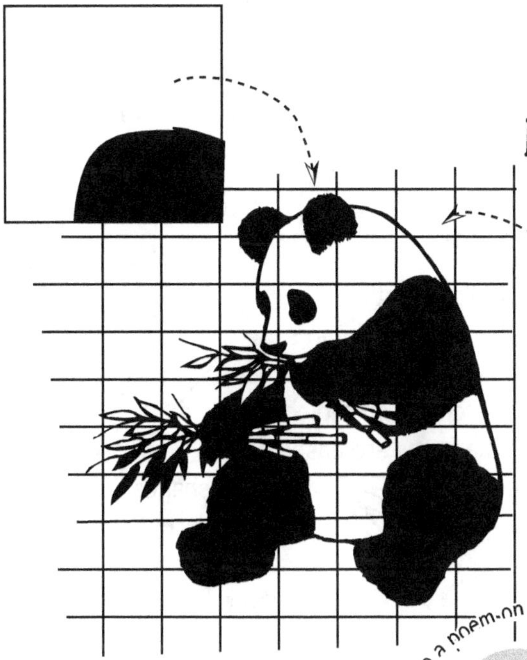

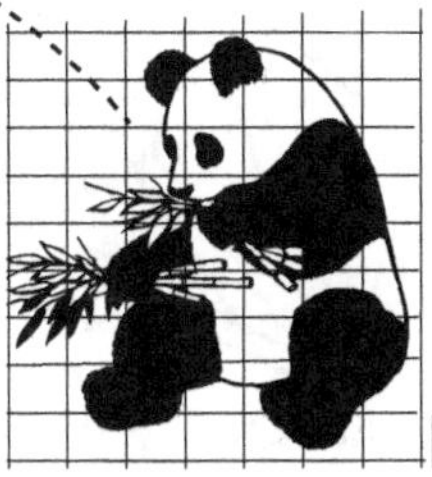

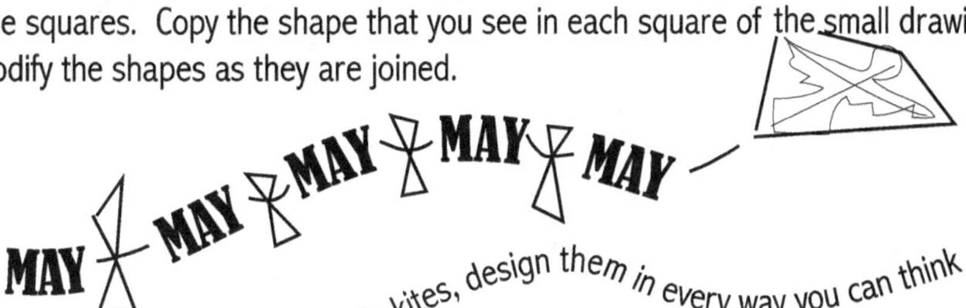

MAY MAY MAY MAY MAY

May is a good time to fly kites, design them in every way you can think of... eagles, dragons, airplanes

Explorer the arts of another culture through the basic elements. It is only through the arts that we can know ancient peoples.
Where would Tutankhamen or Nefertiti be without their artists?

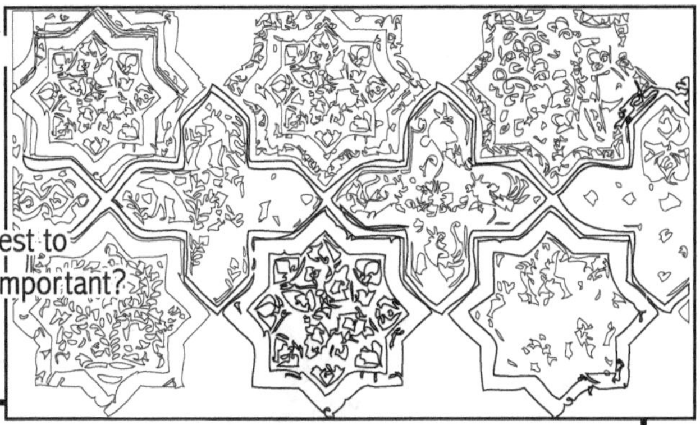

Does that suggest to you that art is important?

Take some balloons, a marking pen. Write a poem on a string.

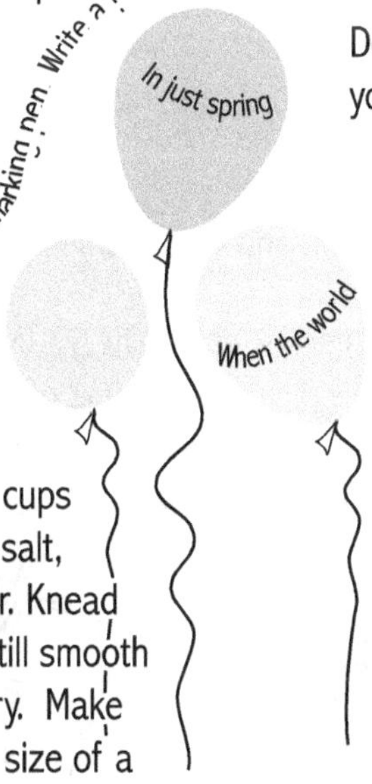

In just spring

When the world

FLOWER CHILDREN

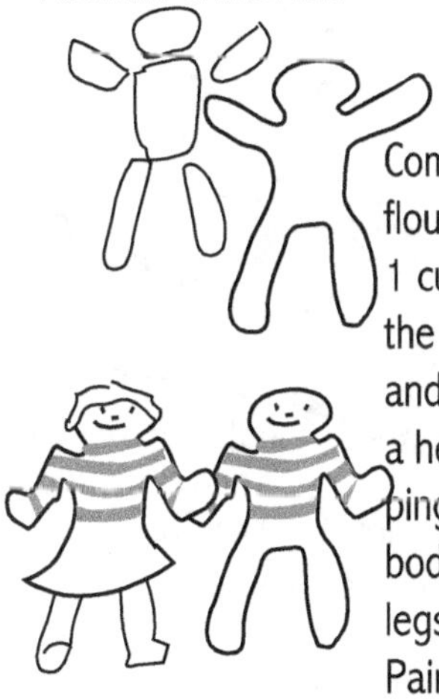

Combine 3 cups flour,1 cup salt, 1 cup water. Knead the dough till smooth and rubbery. Make a head the size of a ping-pong ball, larger for the body. Shape and attach arms and legs. Bake in 275° oven for 1 hour. Paint and decorate. A coat of shellac will help preserve them.

ART 5

- ☐ uses implied edge or contour line
- ☐ uses shape and form rather than line to show mass
- ☐ uses the emotional impact of color
- ☐ uses texture, shape and color as pattern
- ☐ draws with contour and shading tor figure rendering
- ☐ paints, overlays, and blends self-selected monochromatic color schemes
- ☐ prints by intaglio (incising)method
- ☐ can make fabric designs, stitchery, wall hangings, and appliques
- ☐ sculpts by subtractive carving of soap, plaster, and other materials
- ☐ makes conscious judgments of art in product design
- ☐ can discusses rhythm, emphasis, opposition, balance, and sensory qualities In art works
- ☐ discusses conscious judgments in selected works for political, historical and religious meanings

Trace the shadow of things. Change levels, rotate, repeat and overlap shapes. Fill in with shades or tints of colors.

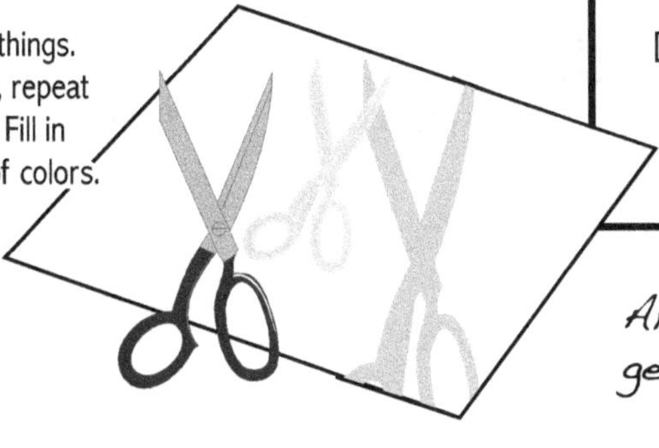

Art should be an essential part of any general educational program.

JUNE

Art Alive

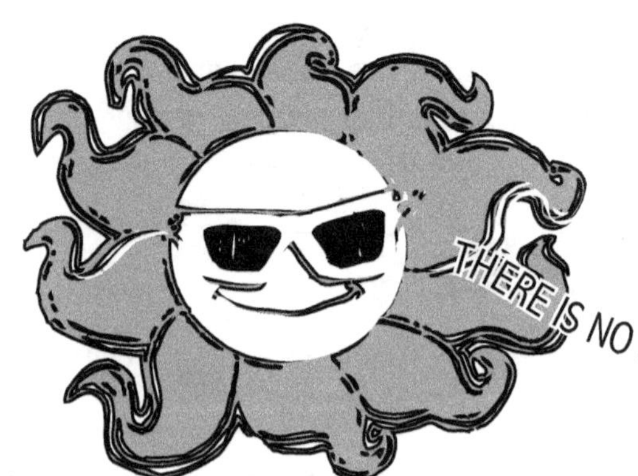

THERE IS NO SEPARATE THING CALLED ART...ONLY QUALITY WAYS OF DOING ANYTHING

Cut out a variety of shapes. Trace around the shapes, overlap them. Color or fill in with texture where the shapes overlap.

Art things you can do on your vacation!
Produce a puppet show
Invent a new musical instrument
Make a design that works with an electric motor
Collect insects, butterflies, rocks, or poems
Print some notepaper or Christmas cards
Create a design for a beach towel
Create a design for a T-shirt

Tightly roll newspapers. fasten papers with tape

Build gigantic backyard sculptures. Use rolled up newspapers fastened with scotch tape. The forms are based on triangular shapes. Fasten the pieces together with tape. Join all of the rolls in large triangles.

With a marking pen on a large sheet of butcher paper creative design using dots. Make some big, some small. Group them, scatter them, and leave some space white.

SUMMER VACATION SQUARES

Draw pictures of some of the things that you would like to do a this summer. They can be imaginary or real.

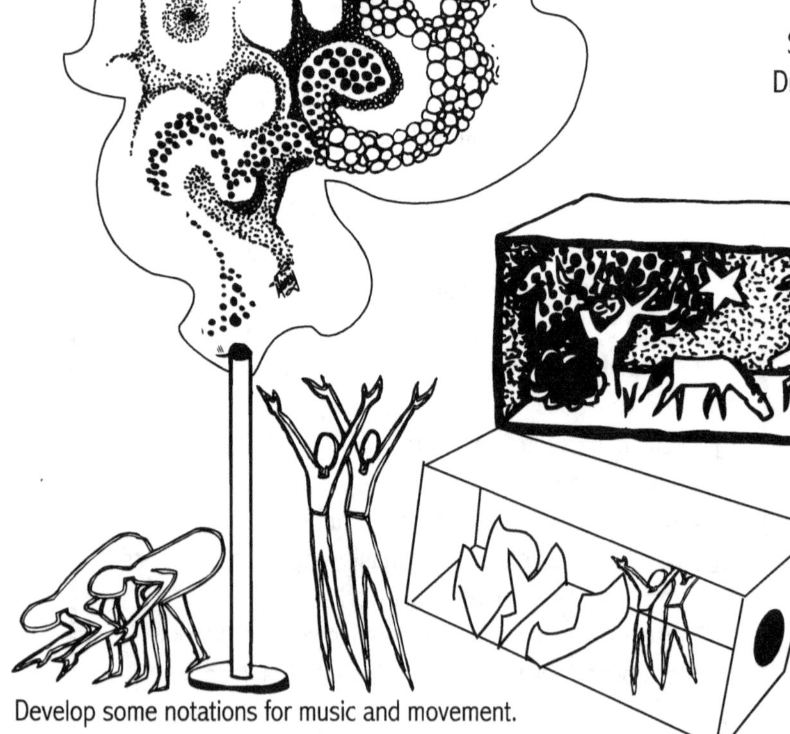

Use old shoe boxes and build dioramas. You can make realistic scenes or sci-fi scenes or Just abstract designs. Use the depth of the box to your advantage with a peep hole in the end. Gives extra depth. Cover the top or the side with colored cellophane. Let the color help your scene.

Develop some notations for music and movement. You need symbols for high, low, fast, slow and whatever else occurs in the music

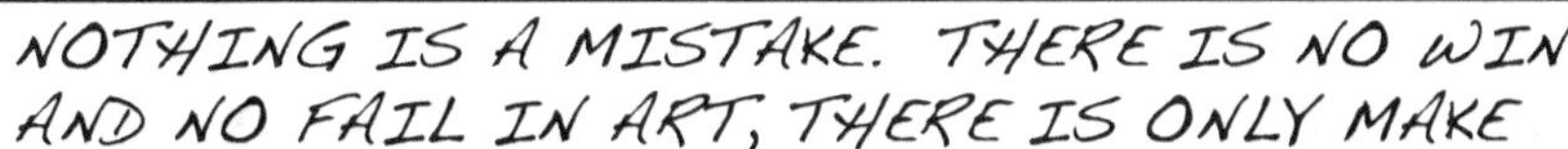

Think up projects that you can do this summer that will involve the elements of art.

RHYTHM

EMPHASIS

OPPOSITION

BALANCE

PERCEPTION

EXPRESSION

JUDGMENT

LINE
TEXTURE
COLOR
SHAPE
SPACE

SIGNS SYMBOLS AND COMMUNICATION

Explore signs in the environment.... TRAFFIC SIGNS...make up signs for keep off the grass, slow, no talking, push etc.

SIGNS OF SUMMER... write, draw, paint.

WHAT IF NO ONE PAID ATTENTION TO SIGNS?

Make some pictures of what would happen if we all ignored the signs. What is the sign for HOSPITAL?

DRAW SOME ICE CREAM CONES

Fill the clones with flavors of colors you cut from magazines.

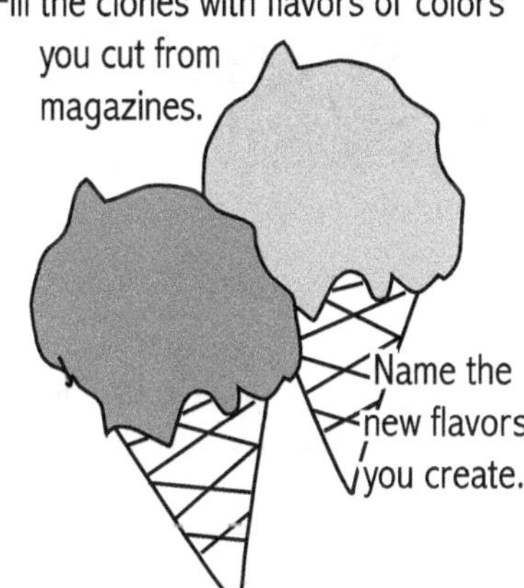

Name the new flavors you create.

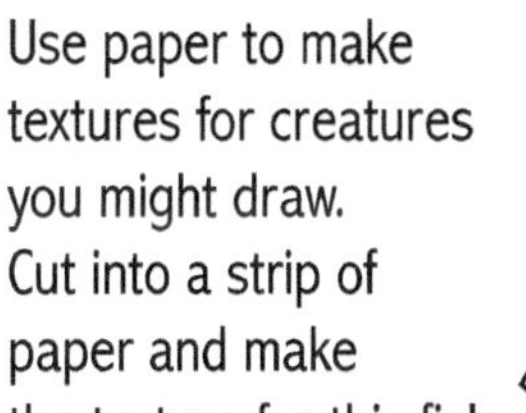

Use paper to make textures for creatures you might draw. Cut into a strip of paper and make the texture for this fish.

How else can you use this texture pattern?

LET FLY YOUR IMAGINATION!

Summer is a good time to fly a kite. Try parafoils, eagles, or just a standard box kite.

Use the repetition of common objects to make a design. Fill the paper with your designs. Try several patterns, try another and then another. Look around you and find an object or objects that you can use.

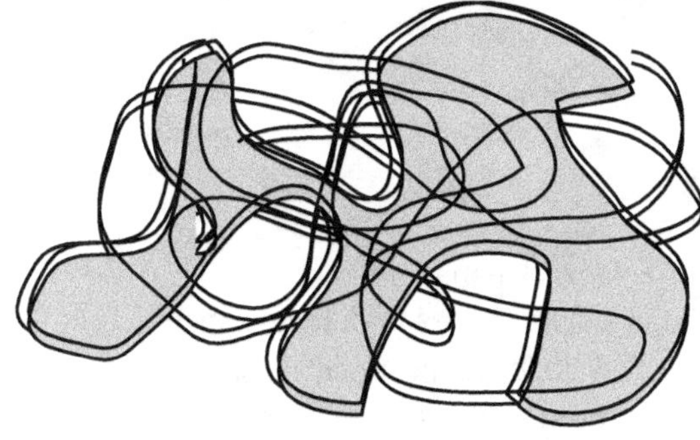

Use left over spaghetti dropped on a Saran film. Fill in areas with paint mixed with white glue. Let dry and peel from film. Use as stained glass windows.

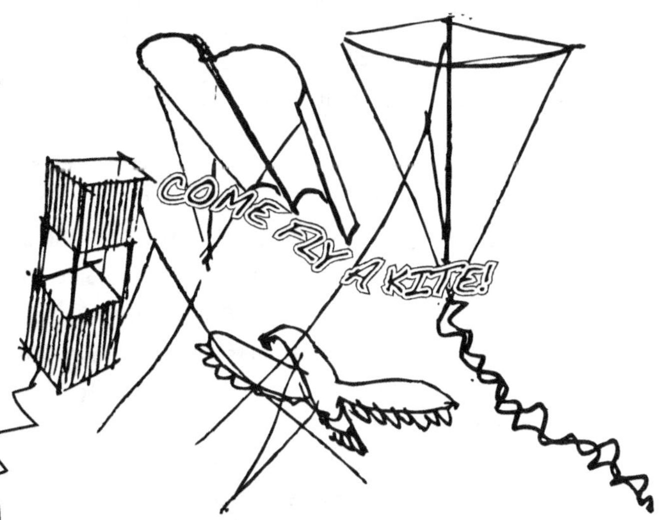

IT'S OK FOR ORANGES TO BE ALL ALIKE, BUT NOT PEOPLE OR ART

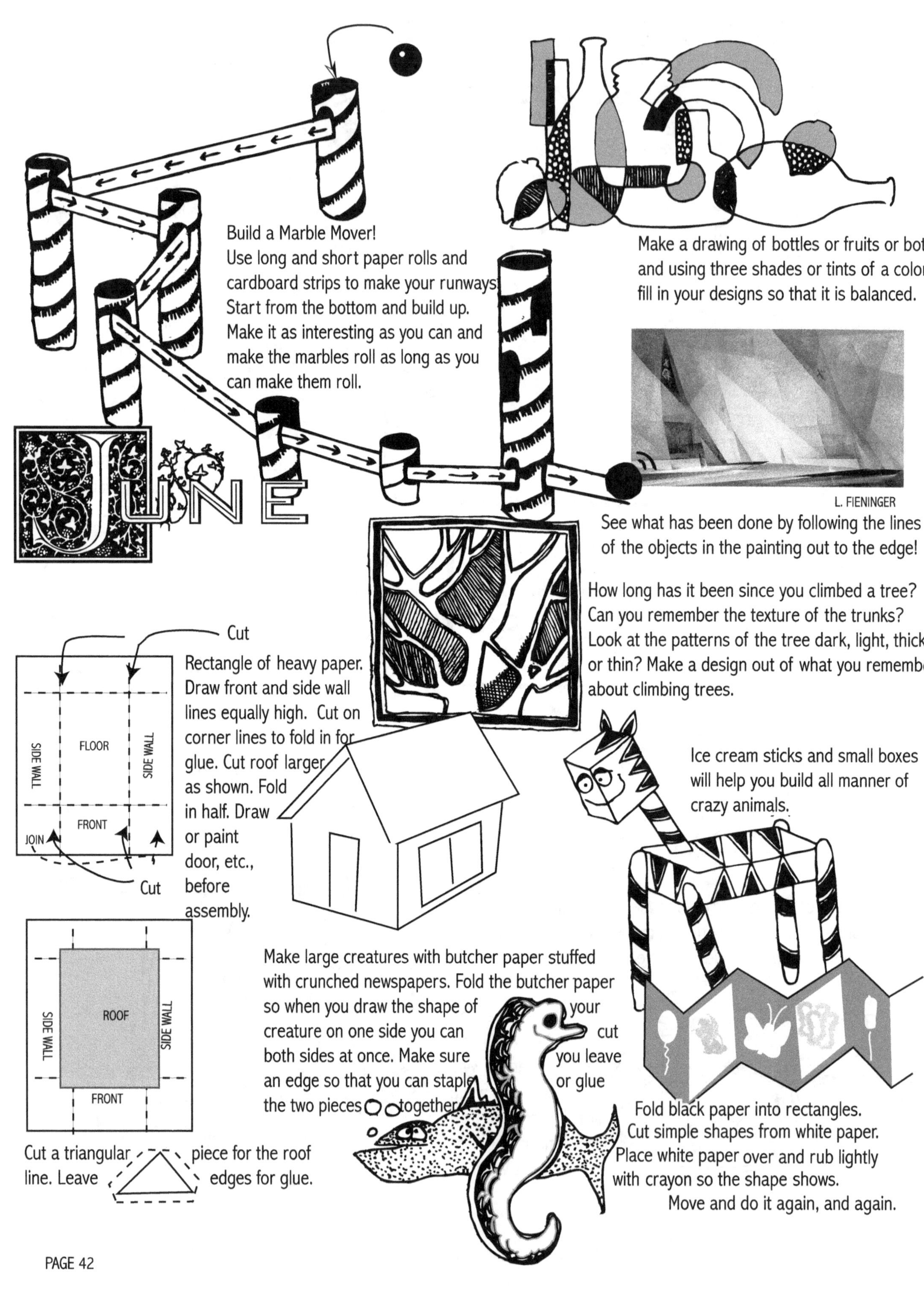
Build a Marble Mover!
Use long and short paper rolls and cardboard strips to make your runways!
Start from the bottom and build up.
Make it as interesting as you can and make the marbles roll as long as you can make them roll.
Make a drawing of bottles or fruits or both and using three shades or tints of a color, fill in your designs so that it is balanced.
JUNE
L. FEININGER
See what has been done by following the lines of the objects in the painting out to the edge!
How long has it been since you climbed a tree? Can you remember the texture of the trunks? Look at the patterns of the tree dark, light, thick or thin? Make a design out of what you remember about climbing trees.
Cut
SIDE WALL
FLOOR
SIDE WALL
FRONT
JOIN
Cut
Rectangle of heavy paper. Draw front and side wall lines equally high. Cut on corner lines to fold in for glue. Cut roof larger as shown. Fold in half. Draw or paint door, etc., before assembly.
Ice cream sticks and small boxes will help you build all manner of crazy animals.
SIDE WALL
ROOF
SIDE WALL
FRONT
Cut a triangular piece for the roof line. Leave edges for glue.
Make large creatures with butcher paper stuffed with crunched newspapers. Fold the butcher paper so when you draw the shape of your creature on one side you can cut both sides at once. Make sure you leave an edge so that you can staple or glue the two pieces together.
Fold black paper into rectangles.
Cut simple shapes from white paper.
Place white paper over and rub lightly with crayon so the shape shows.
Move and do it again, and again.

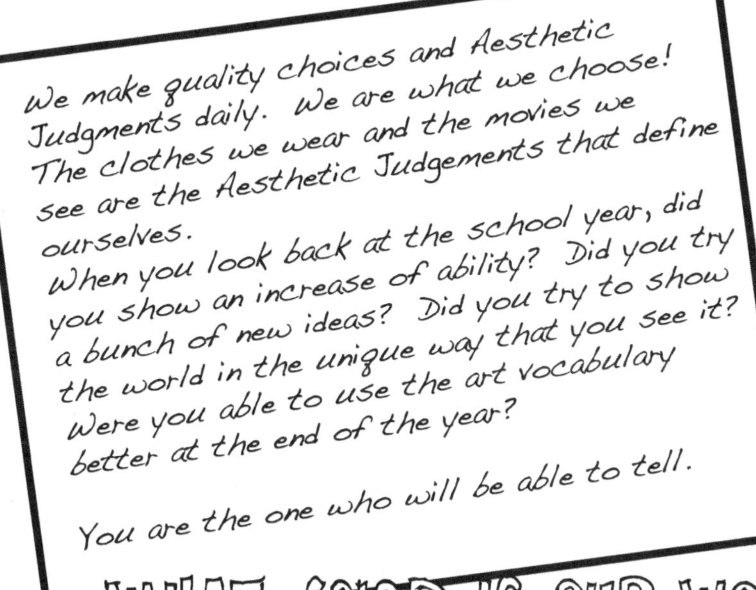

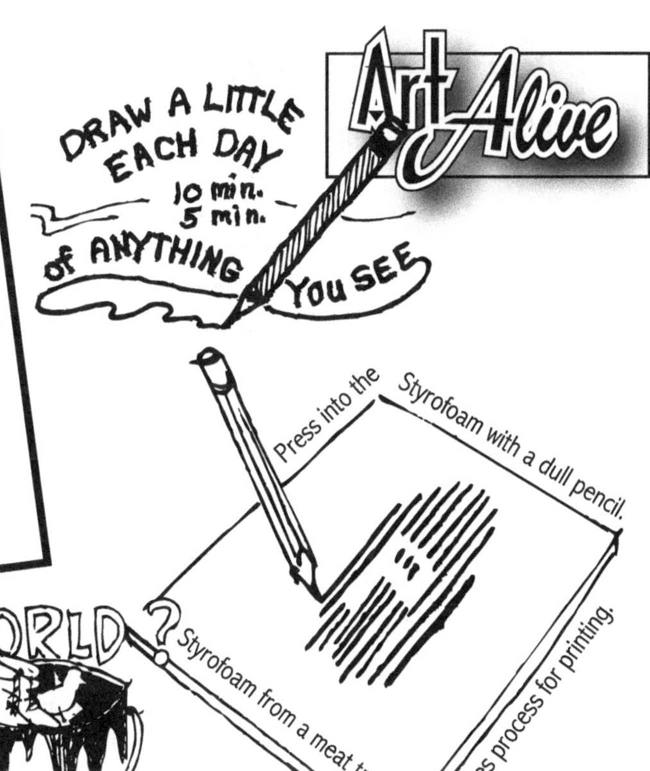

WHAT COLOR IS OUR WORLD?

12"

Yellow Blue Red

Draw and cut out paint buckets about 12 inches tall. Collect from magazines and other sources, the colors that you see that fit in each one.

WATCH FOR.. colors in sunsets and in puddles on oil films and in the soap bubbles and in your friend's eyes, and in bee's wings. Let your heart fly with the sunlight on bright black hair or white tigers running in a jade green forest.

THIS SUMMER FEEL... soft yarn, scratchy beards, slick yellow butter, cool green grass, hot pavement and ask yourself "What texture is a birthday?" or "Is spring soft like a kitten?"

MOST OF ALL... leap high and look and smell and touch and taste and enjoy the world!

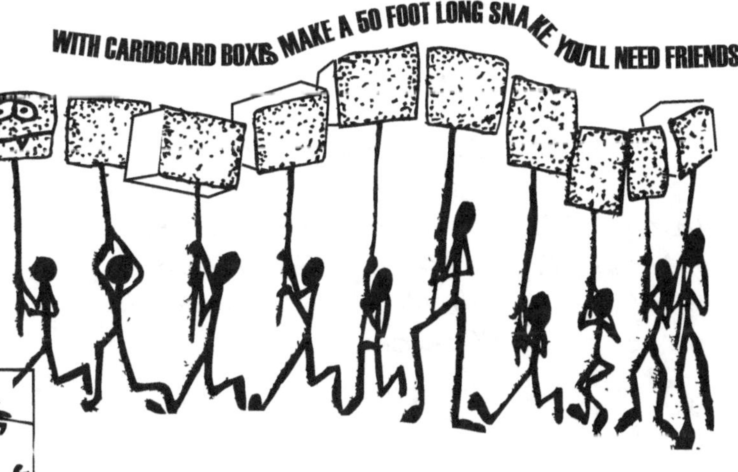

STORY LINE developed a comic strip or a storyboard for a

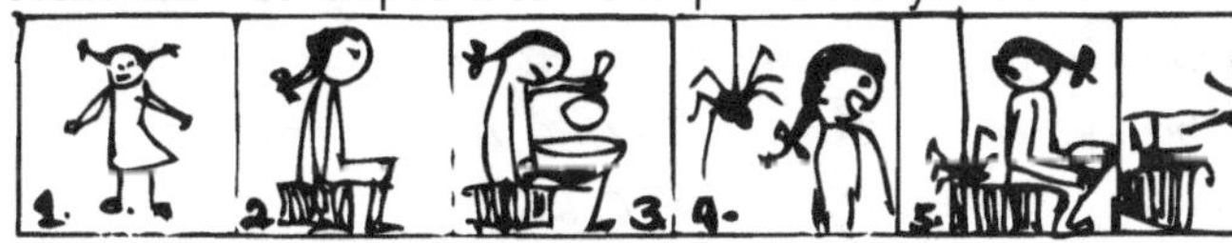

nursery rhyme or other story. You need 1. the character (Ms. Muffett), 2. the setting (the tuffet), 3. the action (along came a spider), 4. the antagonist (the spider), 5. the problem (sat beside her), and 6. the solution (frightened Miss Muffet away)

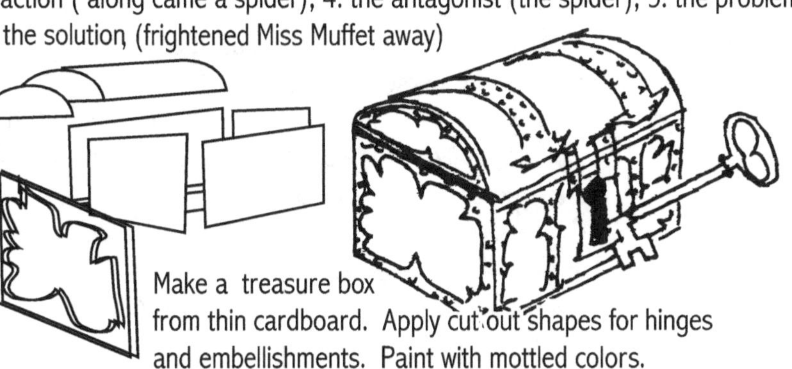

Make a treasure box from thin cardboard. Apply cut out shapes for hinges and embellishments. Paint with mottled colors.

Find new lines, shapes, colors and textures this summer. Keep looking!

Arts And Thinking Skills

OBSERVING: The ability to notice one or more attributes are qualities about an idea or concept.
What is it like? Have you seen anything else like this? What shapes, lines, colors, space, textures do you see? How does the color compared to_____________?

RECALLING: The ability to bring forth information about a previous observation.
What do you remember about it? Do you recall any of the lines, shapes, or color? Are you reminded of anything else by this? Which of the elements help you remember best?

NOTICING SIMILARITIES: isolating one or more attributes in common from two or more dissimilar objects/events.
What else is like this? Tell me what you see that's like _______? What elements are similar to ________? What do they have in common?

NOTICING DIFFERENCES: The isolation of critical elements that point out the dissimilarities between two or more items.
What is different about this? Is that an important difference? Do the differences remind you of anything else? Tell me how you see the differences.

ORDERING: the relating of given objects/concepts according to specified attributes or criteria... Such as small to large.
Tell me why you put this in the middle? What is the pattern you are using? Can you make it in another way? Are you reminded of other patterns by this?

CLASSIFYING: Establishing sets or attribute groupings of events/objects/concepts.
Tell me how you arrange these pictures into your groups? What made you think of that? What qualities made this fit here? Why are these in the same group?

CONCEPT TESTING: to formulate and differentiate between critical and optional attributes and to their cause and effect relationships.
What happened here? Will that always happen? This apple is read and that one is green, why are they both apples? What are things that can go through a keyhole? What attributes would they have?

GENERALIZATIONS: Extend conclusions from observations of one group of sets, attributes, cause and effect and extending those conclusions to other situations.
What is the rule for that? If these fit here will those others? Will this rule always work? What other things does that reminded you of?

MAKING CHOICES: establishing criteria and personal selections based on the criteria.
You selected that painting... can you tell me why? Is this the best shape for your idea? Does that line quality help in your work? What would you change next time? What we thinking about when you did that?

VALUING: Appreciation or cherishing or enthusiasm for an idea, performance or product. Using those elements for personal choices.
*Can you tell me why you are excited by this idea? You like this best of all, can you tell me why?
(Appreciating and cherishing our best shown by modeling..." I really like this." " When I see it I am reminded of another I Like as well."*

TEACHING AN EFFECTIVE LESSON

Any lesson of new material must have a consistent core of presentation. The use of these or similar steps will insure that your students have information presented in logical and complete sequence. It provides an opportunity to learn an idea or process in the correct order and to practice and demonstrate what they have learned before they are asked to apply the learnings on their own.

RATIONALE:

A statement that tells...

1. What the lesson will be and why it is important for the students to learn this lesson. ____________________
2. How this learning will apply to the subject or to other subjects. ____________________

SET STANDARDS:

A statement that tells...

1. What is expected of the students during the lesson. ____________________
2. What materials will be needed by the students. ____________________

LEARNER OBJECTIVE:

A statement that tells...

1. What the students are going to be able to do at the end of the lesson that they can't do now and how you will be able to tell. ____________________

LESSON:

A sequence that...

1. Places instruction in step by step order. ____________________
2. Gives all elements in the order needed that are critical to the learning. ____________________

GUIDED PRACTICE:

An activity confirms for you ...

1. That the students are able to follow the skills you are teaching. ____________________

INDEPENDENT PRACTICE:

An activity that...

1. Allows the students to display on their own the application of the learning. ____________________

CLOSURE:

A question by you that let the students tell you...

1. The lesson was completed as planned. ____________________
2. That they are able to restate or demonstrate the learnings. . ____________________

NOTES

www.ingramcontent.com/pod-product-compliance
Lightning Source LLC
LaVergne TN
LVHW061257100826
845148LV00008B/1162